The Illegitimate Age

Series editors: Adrian Parr and Santiago Zabala

Pointed, engaging, and unafraid of controversy, books in this series articulate the intellectual stakes of pressing cultural, social, environmental, economic, and political issues that unsettle today's world. Outspoken books are disruptive: they shake things up, change how we think, and make a difference. The Outspoken series seeks above all originality of perspective, approach, and thought. It encourages the identification of novel and unexpected topics or new and transformative approaches to inescapable questions, whether written from within established disciplines or from viewpoints beyond disciplinary boundaries. Each book brings theoretical inquiry into a reciprocally revealing encounter with material realities and lived experience. This series tackles the complex challenges faced by societies the world over, rethinking politics, justice, and social change in the twenty-first century.

The Illegitimate Age
Aesthetics and Political Theology
Federico Vercellone
Translated by Robert T. Valgenti

State of Disappearance
Edited by Brad Evans and Chantal Meza

Outspoken
A Manifesto for the Twenty-First Century
Edited by Adrian Parr and Santiago Zabala

Being Vulnerable
Contemporary Political Thought
Arne De Boever

Ecoliberation
Reimagining Resistance and the Green Scare
Jennifer D. Grubbs

Revolutionary Routines
The Habits of Social Transformation
Carolyn Pedwell

Wish I Were Here
Boredom and the Interface
Mark Kingwell

The Illegitimate Age

Aesthetics and Political Theology

FEDERICO VERCELLONE

Translated by Robert T. Valgenti

McGill-Queen's University Press
Montreal & Kingston • London • Chicago

ISBN 978-0-2280-2449-1 (paper)
ISBN 978-0-2280-2450-7 (ePDF)
ISBN 978-0-2280-2451-4 (ePUB)

Legal deposit second quarter 2025
Bibliothèque et Archives nationales du Québec

Printed in Canada on acid-free paper that is 100% ancient-forest-free, containing 100% sustainable, recycled fibre, and processed chlorine-free.

McGill-Queen's University Press in Montreal is on land which long served as a site of meeting and exchange amongst Indigenous Peoples, including the Haudenosaunee and Anishinabeg nations. In Kingston it is situated on the territory of the Haudenosaunee and Anishinaabek. We acknowledge and thank the diverse Indigenous Peoples whose footsteps have marked these territories on which peoples of the world now gather.

Library and Archives Canada Cataloguing in Publication

Title: The illegitimate age : aesthetics and political theology / Federico Vercellone ; translated by Robert T. Valgenti.

Other titles: Età illegittima. English

Names: Vercellone, Federico, author | Valgenti, Robert T., translator.

Series: Outspoken (McGill-Queen's University Press)

Description: Series statement: Outspoken | Translation of: L'età illegittima : estetica e politica. | Includes bibliographical references and index.

Identifiers: Canadiana (print) 20250108119 | Canadiana (ebook) 20250108194 | ISBN 9780228024491 (paper) | ISBN 9780228024507 (ePDF) | ISBN 9780228024514 (ePUB)

Subjects: LCSH: Aesthetics – Political aspects. | LCSH: Political theology. | LCSH: Christianity and politics. | LCSH: Power (Social sciences) – Philosophy.

Classification: LCC BH301.P64 V4713 2025 | DDC 111/.85 – dc23

This book was designed and typeset by Peggy Issenman in 10.5/14 Sabon. Copyediting by Margaret MacQuarrie.

McGill-Queen's University Press
Suite 1720, 1010 Sherbrooke St West, Montreal, QC, H3A 2R7

Authorized safety representative in the EU: Mare Nostrum Group BV, Mauritskade 21D, 1091 GC Amsterdam, the Netherlands, gpsr@mare-nostrum.co.uk

Contents

Foreword

For some time now, there has been talk of a crisis of legitimacy, a reference to the weakening mechanisms of representation threatening the democratic stability of our society. This phenomenology takes on many forms – abstentionism, populism, leaderism – that now converge in the crisis of political parties as regards their primary function of transmitting social needs into politics. But while such analyses are useful, they only scratch the surface of these phenomena and do not penetrate the black box of the democratic deficit, as they miss two fundamental hermeneutic avenues: on the one side, a long-term study of the genesis of this degenerative process; on the other side, the activation of other languages to be placed alongside and intersected with the now-depleted languages of sociology and political science. After all, innovative paradigm shifts occur in every field through the rupture of specialized lexicons and their contamination by grammars with different origins.

Federico Vercellone's *The Illegitimate Age*, appropriately subtitled *Aesthetics and Politics*, moves precisely in this double direction. Based on his unique ability to interweave diverse lexicons – of politics, of theology, and of aesthetics in what Foucault called the "ontology of actuality" – Vercellone's investigation constructs a genealogical journey of particular density that, beginning with the Greek and Latin patristics, and crossing through medieval and modern sources, arrives at the twentieth-century debate over political theology. Situated at the point of confluence, but also tension, between the great interpretative paradigms of modernity – rationalization (Weber), secularization (Löwith), legitimization (Blumenberg) – Vercellone merges their heuristic power with a perspective that benefits from his considerable aesthetic acumen in the fields of Romantic and contemporary art, which produces a particularly original interpretation.

The book begins with the premise that for some time we have been living in a historical and existential condition which the term "crisis" can no longer sufficiently express. Up through the final decades of the twentieth century crises were the means through which economic and political systems were reconstituted and thus avoided collapse. As is known, capitalism itself had for a long time produced its own crises in order to reboot at a more advanced level. In the same way, and not only in Italy, the highly frequent governmental crises served only to redistribute power to the same parties, with the exception of those excluded. But that period, which enjoyed the benefits of successful globalization, was interrupted by apocalyptic flashes that at the start of the new millennium cast their ominous light on Manhattan. The tragic events that have marked the last twenty years – from the 2007 economic crisis to the pandemic, up to the "piecemeal world war" that even tempts an atomic fate – make us think, even more than in normal crises, about true catastrophes in the literal sense of "a change in state." The environmental collapse, for example, seems absolutely catastrophic, now long underway in the age of the Anthropocene, with consequences that are difficult to imagine.

If one had to say what unites these emergencies, despite their heterogeneity, in a single catastrophic drift that projects them well beyond our modern crises, I would say it is the difficulty of finding a *katechon*, by which I mean an immunizing device that can slow down their acceleration. And while the economic collapse – situated between crisis and catastrophe – was able to enjoy the protection of the central banks, and the pandemic collapse was confronted by the last of the biopolitical *katechons*, namely by the vaccine, now the two wars in Ukraine and Palestine are already struggling to find a "withholding power" as they become entwined in a potentially lethal knot. The ongoing environmental disaster, to which humanity now seems resigned, experiences the same lack of an immunizing device – which does not slip into an auto-immune disorder – as we wait for something not entirely different from an "end" to our lifestyle, if not to life itself.

This exhaustion of the *katechon*, and therefore the nightmare of the "end of the world," as de Martino would say, is the centre of gravity for Vercellone's book, which winds along two paths that arrive at the same outcome: on the one hand, an archeology of the figure of the *katechon* which takes us back to the term's first formulation in Paul's Second Letter to the Thessalonians. From then on destined to an irresolvable ambivalence – that of holding back evil while at the same time delaying the coming of the parousia, that is, the second coming of Christ – the concept has preserved its mysterious semantic density throughout its conceptual history, which begins with Irenaeus, Eusebius, and Augustine and ultimately arrives at Schmitt, Taubes, and Benjamin, through the Russians and, in particular, Dostoevsky's *The Grand Inquisitor*. Perhaps nothing expresses a decisive element of the contemporary catastrophe more than Dostoevsky's tale, which marks the departure of every transcendence in modern secularization. This emptying out is what transforms the *mysterium salutis* into the *mysterium iniquitatis*. The inquisitor, destined to succeed Christ in the leadership of men, no longer represents the One, but only himself, depriving the mechanism of representation of its relationship with the Idea, which according to Schmitt is still present in Roman Catholicism – considered, for this very reason, the last refuge of the politician in the world of depoliticization.

Alongside this first path from the past to the present Vercellone places a second, which departs from the present in order to return to the transition at the end of the eighteenth century and the beginning of the nineteenth century, in which early German Romanticism gave birth to a new discourse on the productivity of myth, both aesthetic and political. Not at all a step backwards to an unretrievable origin, myth was, particularly for Schlegel, a formative power which looks forward by emanating a constructive energy capable of injecting new vitality into contemporary reality. In this sense aesthetics rediscovers a political function, or at least an ethical one, which radically overcomes the realm of taste and establishes itself in the world with the intent of changing it. Just as Marx believed that Hegelian philosophy, if reinstated, could transform the relationships between humans, so too early Romanticism spelled out an equally productive mythology through which the past and the present project into the future.

Of course, one might observe that, in general, whenever politics consciously uses myth – and, therefore, a myth, so to speak, that is not natural (if it ever existed) but artificial, of the second order – it has historically belonged to the right. It is true that authors favourable to this use are also present on the left, from the early Sorel to Gramsci, passing through Thomas Mann and Georges Bataille. But one cannot forget that, precisely with regard to the mythopoetic strategy of the latter, Benjamin would show Bataille that he was "working for fascism." That said, I agree with Vercellone. To fight the new mythologies of the right with the blunt weapons of simple rationality, or reasonableness, means losing the battle before it ever begins. Naturally there is myth and myth – those revolutionary ones, or utopian ones, which are not the same as the violent and exclusionary myth of Nazism. In every case it would be difficult, and counterproductive, to think of igniting the spirits for any great project without making recourse to the rich resources of the imagination and the symbolic, even when one is mindful of using such delicate instruments. Beginning with the works of Castoriadis, the instituting character of the imagination is at the centre of the most current research projects.

Adapted to the contemporary condition, Vercellone views such posthumous remythicization as the only possibility left to respond to the catastrophic crisis of legitimacy that has assailed the modern world. Of course, the author is well aware of the fictive nature of possible new myths: Once "God is dead," the disenchantment of the world theorized by Weber becomes irreversible. As Lyotard explained, the grand narratives are spent and Nietzsche's "last man" has no intention of becoming the "superman." And as Hannah Arendt said, following Tocqueville, the thread of tradition has snapped and the past no longer illuminates the future. Both the cyclic time of paganism and the linear time of Christianity have come to an end. If *katechonic* political theology has failed, a similar fate befalls its eschatological and messianic forms. What remains is an empty political theology like the one theorized by Carl Schmitt. As for a trinitarian political theology, to which Vercellone also refers, Erik Peterson had already declared it impossible: How could an economy of salvation based on the distinction between those who rule and those who govern, with the addition of the politically untranslatable figure of the Holy Spirit, serve as the basis for absolute monarchy?

And yet, all that notwithstanding, according to the author not all passages to the future are interrupted. First of all, because all of the historical processes of an epochal nature are intrinsically antonymic – in the sense that they contain, and in fact seem to produce, their own opposite. Is it not precisely globalization that has generated the reactions of new identitarian localisms and even the construction of new walls? Something similar is true for secularization, marked by that phenomenon of the "return of the sacred," which has been observed for some time with mixed results. On the other side, as Marcel Gauchet and Jean-Luc Nancy have explained, isn't Christianity already the religion of the end of religion? All of that – the resistance of the Origin at the moment of its disappearance – is validated by another phenomenon on which Vercellone lingers, namely, the nostalgia for a condition of fullness, or at least of continuity, for the times that, up to a certain point, still linked the generations together through a projectual dimension of existence. Nostalgia and disenchantment, melancholy and terror, are two sides of the same coin, represented in Lars von Trier's film *Melancholia*.

It is precisely in this open gap between nihilism and hope, fear and creative fantasy that, according to the author, one can imagine a resumption of projectuality – not directly political, but primarily aesthetic. Here Vercellone makes recourse to the great repertoire of contemporary art, in addition to the research on morphology conducted by Horst Bredekamp. Only art – and, more generally, mythical, symbolic, imaginary language – can reconstruct the mediation that politics alone is no longer capable of producing. This passage through artistic forms, or through the productivity of images, involves a topological displacement of the transit that leads from society to politics in the double sense: vertically and horizontally. Vertically, an exhausted top-down approach, along with the authority from which it came is replaced by a practice that works from the bottom up, as they say. And horizontally, the reference is not so much to the great "molar" unities – states, nations, peoples – addressed by the new populisms and nationalisms, but rather to the "molecular" articulations, to quote Deleuze, constituted through shared passions gradually generated in relation to specific objectives. Something, it seems to me, closer to new institutionalism than to old sovereignism. To establish life, institutions must already embody a vital impulse. There is a possible relation between Vercellone's aesthetic intuitions and the most recent research into political ontology: Between the verticality of the sovereign paradigm and the pulverization of new philosophical anarchism, there is an entire world comprising institutional creations capable of revitalizing the exhausted forms of contemporary democracies.

Precisely on this last point I would add a final question for the author, leaving the answer completely wide open. In his book, Vercellone compares needs and desires, siding with the former against the latter: The desiring community would be the opposite of a democratic community. Why this is so can be understood from the moment that the desires that we currently live are those mimetic ones produced by the markets of capitalism. As Girard explained, today one desires something not in itself, but only because others desire it. All of the gazes are fixed, in our electronic devices, on the same things, or on the same people, as the phenomenon of leaderism also confirms according to Guy Debord's analysis of the modality of the society of the spectacle. Therefore, the desires are repetitive, compulsive, and, in the final analysis, deadly if the obsessive repetition is the rhythm to which Freud had already linked the death drive. But is desire only this? And, before that, could we contrast it with need, based on a dichotomy that was in vogue some decades ago? Isn't desire also a need without which our life would be closed in upon itself? Could there be a life that is not crossed, and in fact not constituted, by desire? Certainly, all desires today appear to be induced, if not imposed, by the devices that dominate our existence. But then, how should we reinterpret Lacan's claim, which he poses beyond any political theology, that the only real sin is giving ground relative to one's desire?

Roberto Esposito

Acknowledgments

I am very grateful to some friends who have helped to guide this research with invaluable advice that I have incorporated carefully into this work: first of all Horst Bredekamp, Massimo Cacciari, and Roberto Esposito.

Special thanks to Francesca Monateri, to whose research on the history of the *katechon* this book owes a great deal.

A dear thanks also goes to Gregorio Tenti for the help he gave me in the final phase of drafting the text.

The Illegitimate Age

Introduction

The Age of Anti-Utopias

There is an atmosphere that pervades our time and gives the impression that it is out of place – the uneasiness of an era that is going to expire. There is no need to repeat how many times in recent years we have heard that the continuity of time and its character as a project is collapsing. This is already something that has been proposed with the postmodern, which disrupted the intelligibility of linear time through an infinity of intersections and interruptions. Linear time is and was one of the most important vectors of sense, even though it is certainly also one of the most bizarre, as it is wholly derived from messianic time and thus from an idea of time that ultimately reaches it fulfillment. Its impact is obvious insofar as the life of every living thing is a journey from birth to death.

In our time we see a total inversion of the idea of an end, which distances itself from the idea of completion and fulfillment and transforms into a negative and truly final dimension, into the catastrophe that concludes historical time without ushering in a new one. Nonetheless, the "engine" of political theology, however stalled it may be, seems to be timeless and continues to function in our present. Its presence is negative, indicative of a melancholy and a sense of being lost. The vector of time fails at its task: It has become incapable of bringing about the future.

The dimension of time whose project articulates both historical and individual life has thus come to its complete end. This is not a matter of rediscovering the past in the present, or renewing the archetypal, enchanted, or melancholic presence evoked by Ernst Bloch,[1] but also of recognizing concurrent times in the one global time of historical becoming. All of this makes *our* time an epoch that has lost its proper coordinates of sense. Time no longer seems to function like a heuristic process and loses its symbolic effect. Anyone involved in teaching has certainly experienced this firsthand; meanwhile, this very phenomenon produces others that accompany the degeneration of the situation.

If the vector of time loses its immediately projectural character, or if the decline or the inversion of its messianic trajectory causes the very idea of the future to decay, then all of this would be enough to account for the truly imminent and devastating actuality of political theology, which has, not surprisingly, in recent decades also been the subject of intense philosophical reflection in Italy. Time and project are inextricably linked in a panorama that reflects both the *historia rerum gestarum* and also individual history. The structure of individual consciousness inherently believes this mechanism of growth to be positive; in a basic way, this is the meaning of "maturation." Even individual subjectivity introjects the structure of an end understood as a goal. This suggests that the messianic structure plays a pivotal role in the construction of sense for historical as well as for individual existence. And it is precisely from this point of view, on the basis of the intimate connection between historical and individual events (a connection that we could define as structural), that it is possible to grasp profoundly one of the meanings of the process of secularization, which dismantles – at least from this point of view, at least on the historical level – the messianic pattern. All of this clearly produces an interruption and a fracture at the point where the destinies of individual consciousness separate from those of the collective consciousness; for example, Christianity is understood less as a founding myth and simply becomes the realm and site of individual faith.

This creates a fascinating but exhausting reality. The construction of individual sense is shared by that of the collective sense; history assumes a heteronomous direction that cannot be recovered within a mythical structure, which causes even the mythical structure to shatter and give way to a solitary and uncertain consciousness, one forced to construct sense within a bankrupt, or at least failing, mechanism. The chill of rationality and the disenchantment of the world is, after all, precisely this. Consciousness feels like it is living within dead and stiffened structures, like those painted by Casorati according to Gobetti's interpretation.[2] Thus, it does not manage to build its own meaning, such that it now lacks a direction and a conceptual edifice, a reference to a higher narrative. We stand at the edge of an abyss which overturns our original presuppositions. Given that the messianic project, as the mythic-collective horizon, has abandoned the layer of individual consciousness, even this relationship falls into crisis. This is what is known as nihilism.

When the crisis reaches individual consciousness, an overturning of horizons penetrates and infiltrates the imaginary, more severely on the subjective level than on the historical-global one. Here the imaginary is filled with dis-utopias: negative utopias that overturn and confuse the means-end relation, producing a sort of anticipation for the end which approaches a panicked dissolution. The nexus and the site where the goal is constructed, now emancipated from finality, spin around in circles and transform themselves into what has been defined as instrumental rationality, a sort of illogical logic that promotes its own formal ends, turning back on itself in a schizophrenic way, by now forgetful of its ancient totalizing and global vocation. We therefore enter the age of anti-utopias. Its structure, as the vocation of late modernity, is the subject of this book. The decline of the messianic message thus produces the highest form of contradiction: the idea of an anti-utopian modernity. The new age par excellence, the age dedicated to the future, is also what collides with the most profound overturning of its own paradigms of sense; and, above all, it cannot and does not manage to fully restrict the functioning of the engine that gives it structure. This engine overturns its own axiological horizon without modifying its temporal direction. The dreamed for and evoked end, the coveted completion and even a "messianic neurosis,"[3] which was mentioned in the early centuries of the Christian era, is overturned in a counter-finality, in a negative finality that produces nightmares of the total catastrophe evoked by the anti-utopian dream, much as the end goal of fulfillment was coveted in the early Christian centuries.

Katechon

After all, the Christian story has always included some element of withholding. The announcement of the return has always been withheld by some event that acts as an impediment to the history of salvation. The waiting for the return of the Messiah was beset by obstacles that thwarted its coming to pass. In Paul's Second Letter to the Thessalonians, this shows itself and is articulated in a form that remains unchanged for nearly two millennia. In one of the most famous passages (2 Thessalonians 2:1–12) Paul warns us to be on the lookout for false messiahs and imposters who try to portray themselves as the true God, or – secondarily – as the apostle who has returned. He also says that there is a *katechon* (the term is used in the text both in its substantive and adjectival forms), "a power that withholds" the advent of the *mysterium iniquitatis.* When it overcomes this obstacle, the *mysterium iniquitatis* will manifest itself under the form of all sorts of spells and pseudo-enchantments, only to be annihilated by the Messiah who will finally establish his kingdom.

The term *katechon* appears numerous times in the context of Greek culture, among them in Plato (who, in the *Apology of Socrates*, identifies the protagonist as the *katechon*). But with Paul a completely different history unfolds.[4] First of all, it reveals a fundamental element that establishes the *katechon* in its quality as the "form that withholds," *forma qui tenet* according to the

Latin Vulgate tradition. It articulates the history of salvation as a particular itinerary whose route also includes detours. There are necessary steps: for example, the fact – underlined by one of the most important figures in the debate over the *katechon*, Erik Peterson – that it is also necessary for the evangelical message to reach the gentiles after it has reached the Jewish people.[5] In any case, and regardless of the historical and philological significance of these interpretations, the course of the history of salvation, messianically oriented, does not follow a linear trajectory, but must perform a circumnavigation in order to reach its completion.

The narration of this story, at least briefly – which covers a very long temporal axis from Paul to the Greek and Latin patristics, through the meaningful moments of medieval thought, to the Reformation, and then reaching Dostoevsky, Carl Schmitt, and finally our present – will therefore involve accounting for those moments of stability within the messianic story that have necessarily delayed it. Luther's words, which expound upon the "thy Kingdom come" of the Our Father to affirm that if the end of the world were to come tomorrow he would still plant his apple tree sapling,[6] demonstrate the need for relatively stable time within the messianic story. This holds until the need for stability no longer supports the messianic call and cancels it; while the institution that takes its place is no longer the representative of the one legitimate power but will become the *auctoritas* itself – which it should restrict itself to represent. In this way, the substitute delegitimates its own power. Furthermore, insofar as the representative replaces what he represents, he assumes the aspect of the double who wishes to take the place of the legitimate authority, thus in some way realizing Paul's prophecy.

Not surprisingly, the *katechon* has been interpreted, in the course of its history, either as the empire or as the Church of Rome – the institutions that provided moments of rest in the dizzying passage of the time of salvation. They are the principle of historical time and they manifest powerful aesthetic connotations in that they behave like the epiphanies of a God who legitimates their existence but is never embodied by or fully present in them. The power of the *katechon*, precisely by virtue of its aesthetic connotation, is therefore never theocratic and does not have a totalitarian face, at least in the sense that allows differences to grow and mature under its umbrella. The epiphanic structure of power, so construed, in many ways constitutes the model of a legitimate power that does not depend on itself but that has a transcendent foundation and, therefore, is not arbitrary. When this structure is eventually disregarded, it happens because it achieves infinite aestheticization rather than its successful form and representation. This, ultimately, is the principle and the root of modern alienation.

It is as if our time – here we see the current import of the *katechon* – were to live through an exasperating event which gives rise to an intense nostalgia, not so much for the structure of legitimate power, but for the representation shared across forms of power (whether they are monarchic or democratic), such that we now fully experience the form of the double who can no longer represent the original. That brings about a disorientation of the subjects in play, who search for an identity that no longer speaks and has tried to hide itself in unfathomable recesses, for reasons that we are going to consider. These lost and surrogated identities become the principal goods of the market, as the populist crowds testify in a degenerate form. What is proposed is a new form of capitalism, one that no longer, in a Marxist sense, produces goods whose use value is transformed into exchange value. In this Marxist lens, the object is initially neutral and only later assumes a qualitative definition, a value that derives from the market and its inputs, and from which it is nevertheless alienated. Now, on the contrary, we are dealing with a dimension where goods are *identity itself*, and, therefore, never neutral. We are dealing with a market that recalls – perhaps from afar and somewhat imperfectly – the *mysterium iniquitatis* of Paul: what gives fictitious identities to subjects who are clothed in borrowed garments and have lost any authenticity. This *market of identities* is characterized by admittedly aesthetic categories: beyond that of the lookalike, the categories of kitsch and prestige will be considered in the sixth and final chapter of this book.

The connection that joins aesthetics and politics is absolutely central to these considerations. On the one hand, the event of the *katechon*, even in its absence, even when defined as a blind archetype that neither emanates nor reflects the light needed to maintain its valence, highlights and introduces some fundamental elements.[7] Not incorrectly, Schmitt notes: "As it was in the 1500s or in the 1800s, we are always in the Christian *aion*." He continues: "Always in agony, and every essential event is only a question of the *katechon*, that is to say, of the one who withholds, *qui tenet nunc*."[8] By reaffirming the actuality of political theology, Schmitt reminds us that we are still in the Christian era precisely because the *katechon*, if only negatively, maintains the integrity of its force as the dizziness of the void and the call of the archetype.

One might ask how to proceed, even on the political level, when transcendence fails, when the foundation flounders and can no longer ensure its current power and its structures. Faced with the fragmentation of public opinion into countless streams and diverse identities that struggle to organize themselves into a unified sovereign body, one might ask, precisely in the void of the *katechon*, if there could be a politics that renounces it, that no longer understands the system of representation on the basis of a top-down model, but instead on one that is bottom-up, and thus according to a representation of groups (which is not to say that they are exclusively of power) that like atolls in an ocean comprise the global world.

1

The Anti-Utopian Age

We Have Never Been Postmodern

Questioning our own time is always also questioning the places where we dwell. To be *a time*, even the most tragic epoch must be habitable and be recognized as such by its inhabitants. The Anthropocene, the epoch in which nature is or seems to be completely at the mercy of human demands, is also the epoch that has erased its defining characteristic – habitability. In many ways, the Anthropocene appears to its own inhabitants as an indefinable epoch, if not an uninhabitable one. It is an epoch of the end, a time that produces and feeds off high and low anti-utopias, one whose very presence intensifies rhythmically as we move closer to today. From *Apocalypse Now* to *The Thin Red Line*, from *Dylan Dog* to Anselm Kiefer's *The Seven Heavenly Palaces*, we are always dealing with a modernity that projects its own end into a near future without ever actually undergoing it. It is, therefore, an epoch marked by a saturated imaginary, ever more a prisoner to the irony and the anguish of its inhabitants. From irony to anguish and anguish to irony defines the unique swing of the pendulum, an oscillation complementary in its outcomes, which are summed up in the dissolution of projectuality and of the future itself.

Our time still stands out as messianic, even though its horizon of sense is overturned: The end is no longer the coveted *telos*, the extinguishing of time in its regeneration, but an imminent implosion. In contrast to the ancient idea of the end as the ultimate and definitive *end*, which raises humanity and creation from this valley of tears and delivers them to a total regeneration, there remains only the exorcizing of anguish, constantly projected on the imaginary plane. The end is now evoked to make us comfortable with our own disappearance while simultaneously holding it off. It is thus a time that is lived neurotically as the end times, even if it is oriented toward its own implosion rather than toward the apocatastasis. Instead of the Messiah, it covets an end to the anxiety that runs through it; but it is also a time of nostalgia, always on the hunt for an identity to be rediscovered in a past that bundles, almost into a neat little package, food, fashion, modern antiques, dialects – all the things that are part of an immediate past we already miss.

A Truly Secularized Modernity?

The outcome of modernity is therefore, to some extent, the opposite of that secularizing vocation which seems to distinguish many "classic" theories of modernity. It is well known that secularization has produced some unexpected results, in many cases leaving behind the Weberian "disenchantment of the world" and awakening what Hans Joas defined as *Die Macht des Heiligen*, the power of the sacred.[1] In other terms, the process of rationalization imposed by capitalism is modified in its very way of being and loses the features of an anonymous and depersonalized experience: Capitalism has become a form of life, and it has done so by aestheticizing itself. It aestheticizes goods by making them symbolic, markers of status, of place, of identity. Its products increasingly escape the anonymity of Marxian exchange value, becoming unique and thus always less exchangeable with each other. A domestic object, like a refrigerator covered with photos and magnets, or even objects of luxury or art, are always personalized objects, "low intensity mythologies"[2] that reflect a time anxious about knowing itself. That, of course, in many ways contradicts the Marxian paradigm of alienation.[3]

A rather intense mixture of motivations runs through modernity and its developments ever since the renewal of the debate over postmodernism, precisely when it seemed that the question would have come to a definitive end. To invoke and summarize the title and thesis of one of Bruno Latour's famous books,[4] we could also say that *we have never been postmodern*. Modernity, with all of its emancipatory aspirations, was never really interrupted, even if it had been in crisis. On closer inspection, the entire debate on postmodernity belonged, after all, to the crisis of modernity itself.[5] The postmodern – its idea of the end of history (or of a linear narrative on the development of our time that enables a bridge to be constructed between the present and the past), its idea of a multiplicity of styles that weave the shared fabric of society and of social coexistence, all mixed together in a present without a future that aggregates everything in the *hic et nunc* – is not in reality distinct from modernity but simply its collapse. On the other hand, it is in the context of a conservative mentality that the idea of the end of history advocated by Fukuyama arises.[6] The dystopian imaginary – as we will see more clearly later on – makes up part of this conservative *reverie*. Modernity no longer accelerates and is no longer secular time as the inheritor of messianic, Romantic, and Enlightenment time together, devoted to a redemptive and regenerative end; it is instead unmoving, stagnant, and ubiquitous time in which we still manage to live and in which an exorbitant number of events occur, too numerous to count.

Postmodernity is the paradoxical epoch which questions the very capacity of time to create order, to be a vector of sense. At the same time, it is the age that has erased the lack of symmetry in historical time, displayed in an exemplary way by a work that practically inaugurates the postmodern: Robert Venturi's *Learning from Las Vegas*.[7] The postmodern erased that inchoative presence of the past in the present, the dissymmetry of time that, as Bloch had shown, engages the utopian function. It is the implosion of the modern, which had made the future its own vector of sense. The chaos of an infinite multiplicity of styles no longer signifies, as it did in the chaos of the German Romantics,[8] the beginning of everything, but instead its end.

The postmodern thus develops a sneaky gaze: Behind the reconciliation with the world and the end of utopias looms the menace of anti-utopia, the omen of the now imminent end. The postmodern is the most complete decommissioning of the messianic identity of the modern, in favour of what Nietzsche, in *Thus Spoke Zarathustra*, defined as "the last man." And so begins a general crisis of identity that involves both the epoch and its sense, its principles of legitimacy and foundation. Its patina of indetermination, of plurality, of behaviours and styles hints at the deeply aestheticizing atmosphere of this event.

Often it is not clear what aestheticism really means, or what motivates its actions. A good deal lies behind the surface of aestheticism: grafted onto and alongside its aesthetic reasons one also finds political and social problems of great importance. When one speaks of an aesthetic tendency, to return to what I was saying above, one also speaks of a transformation of the idea of the end and of the end itself: If the West has long been dominated and, in fact, consumed by its desire for the end as apocatastasis, realization, and completion – as the messianic anxiety of the first centuries of Christianity attests – now everything seems to be overturned.[9] Anxiety about the end and the Messiah's return is replaced by its opposite: the panicked fear of the imminent end that overturns the messianic plan and turns utopia into anti-utopia. The subject is disarmed in the face of the impending storm. Responsibility is dismissed.

The passage through anti-utopias is consubstantial with modernity and its end. It is a constitutive part of its complacently negative imaginary, which contrasts with the messianic roots of the modern.[10] The impending end arrives from the known that has become unknown, from the monster that is in us and that emerges unexpectedly in an infinite theory of characters that runs from Frankenstein's monster to Dylan Dog.[11] The fact that this end is total and irredeemable evokes, in contrast, the longed-for end of the first centuries of Christianity.

The terrorizing end, evoked as the suspension of anguish, thus evokes the withholding. This is how the anti-utopian modernity recalls the *katechon*, the withholding power mentioned by Paul in his Second Letter to the Thessalonians, however without managing to create it – no matter how much messianism evokes the end as fulfillment. The abyssal horror of an end that exists only as dissolution replaces the end coveted by messianic hope, which was inherited from a newly born modernity (which early German Romanticism embodies, like a gem, in its purest form). Our own time has grown ever more habituated to the overturning of the idea of an end, which – to reiterate the thesis – loses any theological-messianic connotation to become the symbol of the impending catastrophe. Anti-utopian dreams are not simply symptoms of an age in crisis, but rather have a precise functionality within the scope of this supposed or real crisis. The apocalyptic dream does not completely disappear from our history: it has simply changed its plan radically, manifesting (also) as the desire for the end that eases the anguish about the future.

It is then very important, in this context, to clarify a misunderstanding that infects all reasoning: The anxiety over the evoked and dreaded end, the panicked fear for the loss of the world is in reality an anxiety over *our* end. An anthropic point of view, both ideological and vaguely comical, makes its way in these catastrophic thoughts. Briefly, and to express it very simply, the anxiety for the end of the world manifests the fear over the destiny of the human species and its life on this earth; upon closer inspection, it does not actually concern the end of all life on this planet, nor even the end of the planet itself. The anxiety over the total end amplifies, in a cosmic key, something that is rather finely detailed. The properly ethical side of the question, which would otherwise remain concealed, can be exposed only by emphasizing that the end of the world is in reality *our* end. Only by clarifying this side can one then change the discourse, lifting off its ideological veil so that something unexpectedly simple can be understood, namely, that our responsibility to our planet and our future is at stake. Regarding the general state of a culture, this awareness certainly has a rather remarkable ethical-political significance and keeps us from remaining ensnared by the dizzying allure of negative utopia.

Aestheticization

What then is aestheticization? It is evoked often, such that its meaning is almost taken for granted. Aestheticization coincides with a change in the orientation of the gaze. We are dealing with an epoch that has increasingly emphasized the function of the gaze in its ability to inquire and illuminate, to tolerate shadows – as Victor Stoichita has shown in the *Sherlock Effect*[12] – and, in the end, to produce a sort of reality with a retinal structure, founded on a gaze that explores, discovers, and desires. The primacy of the gaze carries along the organization of all the other senses, including touch, traditionally entrusted with the experience of reality understood as friction and resistance. What could be defined – if you will excuse the clumsy neologism – as the ocularization of reality has become a premise and a consequence of our social and cultural organization.

It would be a misrepresentation to understand this experience – as occurs in a relatively long tradition stretching from Debord to Baudrillard and then to the *Truman Show* – as if it were under the effect of an illusionistic and ideological dematerialization of reality, whose performativity and power is, moreover, fully certified. One could instead say that what takes place is a transfer of reality from its physical consistency to one that is different and has a psychic nature that is continually transmitted by new media. The gaze activates desire insofar as it moves away from the object, thus postponing the satisfaction of possession; this places a new emphasis on desire through a neurotically reiterated mechanism. Aestheticization thus coincides with the *ocularization of experience*, which transforms its quality by rendering it monosensed or one-way *à la lettre* and directing it toward the current regime of gazes, that is, toward what is defined as the society of the image. This is not born out of nothing, but from a modification of and in the structuring of human needs, which is at the same time the premise and the outcome of a radical modification of the quality of capitalistic production: what Gernot Böhme has defined "aesthetic capitalism."[13]

We are dealing with a universe in which goods have been aestheticized, while the gaze upon them is loaded with an expectation of satisfaction from afar, more or less remotely sexualizing. In this way, images become a depository of expectations for satisfaction and happiness independent of the effective possession of the object, which is thus fully aestheticized.[14] From the point of view of its ontological status, the image assumes an atmospheric quality:[15] It is both a narration and a world-environment. The image (or at least this type of image) is therefore much more than itself and constantly contains within itself a narrative extension – this provides, from the beginning, an immersive dimension where desire takes root in an identity and likewise identity takes root in a desire. To possess the object is, in this way, not only an enlargement of the self, but also, and perhaps above all, its potentially reassuring identification with, and saturation by, an infinite narration. Not surprisingly, food is sold as if it were art and art as if it were luxury jewels, each identified primarily with its histories and with the vicissitudes of its provenance (as Slow Food attests). One need only read the pages of the *Financial Times*' weekend supplement once to notice immediately that good taste, as a system of the subject's ability to recognize who belongs to the same class, is identified with the history of dwelling, and likewise, the history of dwelling with good taste (this is the sense of *luxury* and of antiques).

There is perhaps no work of art more meaningful, in this regard, than Marcel Duchamp's final work, *Étant donnés*, on which the artist laboured for more than twenty years. A work in its own way grandiose and truly diagnostic, it reflects on the end of art or of the artistic object that was already loudly rejected, with a tone more mocking and amused, by his work *Fountain*. In *Étant donnés*, Duchamp asserts moreover that the aesthetic space is now that of reality. But at the same time he shows that reality is no longer "what it was once upon a time" (with all due respect to the nostalgia of "new realism"). "The real world," taking up Nietzsche's famous expression which has provoked many useless polemics, has not "become a fable" or illusion, but has instead assumed a new consistency and a performativity on a level that privileges the primacy of seeing over that of touch. The ancient "tactile" consistency of reality is transferred into another modality, one that is "ocular." This does not mean, however, that the real is no longer real in all its performativity and power.

Duchamp achieves all of this in *Fountain*, placing the famous urinal in an expository context to create a shocking effect (for the time); however, in *Étant donnés*, he works more meditatively to place us in a speculative space that is decidedly metaphysical, almost as a meta-reflection on the state of art. This work, much less known than the earlier work, constitutes its ideal *pendant* and completion: It places the spectator on one side of a peephole to gaze onto a scene, both chilling and obscene, of a woman (a rubber mannequin), presumably murdered and still bleeding, lying naked in the brush with her genitals in the foreground. The orientation of the gaze – which ironically invokes the Albertine window principle of every reality *quae fictio*[16] – is here forcibly sanctioned, affixed on a contradictory reality, revolting but also secretly appealing, totally private and in some way seductive due to its secret nature, which arouses contradictory and promiscuous feelings, being both obscene and repugnant. The gaze is polarized and lives in solitude, backing away but also desiring to get closer and close together; it is translated into the desire to see, and, in a secret, private, and intimate inclination, weaves together the profiles of both the voyeur and the detective. It constitutes an ironic movement and a true unveiling. The intimate gaze becomes public and investigative, and the public gaze is made intimate. As also occurs with the great collectors, the public sphere is mixed up with the most intimate desire, with the curiosity to see without being seen inside a space that is, moreover, only visual and thus impossible to travel through. The public space in this way becomes a morbid space, in which the desiring gazes which ask for the recognition and self-recognition of themselves and of their status intersect in an extreme, almost tragi-comic competitive dissymmetry.

Goods, from their inception always already aestheticized, today forcefully repeat the movement of approaching and distancing seen and almost exemplified by Duchamp, as if to solidify the *iter* in aestheticization. This happens because goods increasingly become connotations and amplifications of the self, as if sanctioned by an amplified identity, as occurs in an exemplary way with fashion and luxury goods. Aestheticization engages and almost becomes enmeshed with the subject's desire: It emphasizes and exalts the self's desire for amplification, which is renewed in a very interested and competitive contemplation. It is a true conflict of gazes where identity is put on the line (this is particularly evident in the case of luxury). This is a paradoxical but total overturning of Kant's aesthetic awareness that speaks – as is well known – of an aesthetic pleasure purely devoid of interests. Pleasure, which is alien to every contact with the object, is in this case interested. It does not derive from a propensity toward the object itself; rather, it depends on the reverberation of its image on the subject, experienced in the public space as a certification of identity. Here we enter the paradox of our times. The distance from the object, its image, has become the paradoxical condition not only of desire (as it has probably always been), but also of its satisfaction. The definition of this type of image is completely ambiguous. It hardly corresponds to that of an idol, as its consistency is not that of the object of adoration and worship but, instead, is based essentially on its subjective reverberation.

The political ramifications of these processes – which have already been foretold for centuries, already in early modernity in visual mechanisms like the camera obscura[17] – are rather remarkable. This produces a sort of approval of gazes, connected to their forceful orientation toward the same point of focus, to their union in the same desiring and approving look. This look is also competitive, since it is always directed toward the same objective, regardless of subject. It is a phenomenon that contemporary technologies repeat on the most diverse platforms, for example in videogames where the action unfolds from a first-person perspective. What is defined here is a place subjected to the gaze, a desiring community that in our world increasingly replaces the human *societas*, the *Gesellschaft*, the democratic community of Rousseauean memory.

The approval of gazes, on the other hand, coexists with a condition of the radical dissymmetry of desire, which seeks out the most diverse images and, on their behalf, creates compartmentalized systems of self-recognition within the global universe. This means, in the final analysis, that communal symbols no longer exist or are becoming increasingly scarce, beset by a true invasion of idiosyncratic symbols used to identify groups and communities. The authentic community of gazes is interrupted, breaking the link with symbols and common images that – as Marie-José Mondzain has shown – institutes democracy itself. Connected as it is to its luminous evidence, the image deposited in the relation of the *imago* with the invisible loses its *logos*, decaying into a total, almost pornographic evidence.[18] Thus it is the invisible, not the visible, which must be shared, as Mondzain observes in *Le commerce des regards*, where she writes: "Judgment and choice, and the idea of life, death, and freedom within a culture, always play with the definition of that which cannot be portrayed and with its inscription. To see both is not to share a vision because no one will ever see what another sees. To see together is to share the invisibility of a sense. Empathic sharing is a political question that requires the communal construction of a critical gaze. In this way the field of a critical market of gazes is opened."[19]

Democracy and the Community of Desire

The desiring community takes shape and replaces the democratic *societas*, profoundly modifying the latter's characteristics and contents, such that

- it now directs its gaze upon a *visible visible,* which we can define as a visible without background, and not upon an *invisible visible,* a visible endowed with a background. The background indicates the provenance and constitutes, namely, the genetic, chaotic, indeterminate element which precedes the determinable, which is revealed as the result of a process of choices – as a *decision*;
- it no longer grounds its own being on the abstract community that is realized in the sovereign body. This latter is a community – Cassirer's hypothesis about Rousseau is right[20] – that does not depend on the physical or psychological characteristics of its own members, but instead constitutes an abstraction from and of the individual subject devoted to being a participant in a single sovereign body, beyond the asymmetries and differences between empirical subjects.

The democratic community is founded upon the principle of an abstract symmetry among concrete individuals, which forms the contradictory foundation of democratic humanism: the idea of an equal value among ideal subjects, however absolute those differences might be in flesh and blood. Individuals who, distinct from real ones, lack any idiosyncrasies, symmetrical and equal among themselves – at least in a certain context regarding their establishment as a sovereign body and thus as subjects of political decisions. The democratic subject reclaims the classical model as the ideally nude individual, related to the god or to the athlete, *purely human*, to express itself as a follower of the eighteenth-century religion of the human.[21] It is, in other words, *an individual of principle*, and thus ideally equal to all others. On the aesthetic level, this ideality is protected by the nude, the symbol of an equality that precedes every cultural process. The nude individual is thus in some way the *homo democraticus*. And so the melancholic, impossible ideal of a humanity that no longer exists[22] lurks in the background; whereas today – it is only a synecdoche, no matter how meaningful – one no longer knows the nude and its seductions, but only bodies that are marked from the beginning, whether it be with tattoos or a pacemaker.

What is defined as the society of the image is not a society of subjects who are ideally equal among themselves. We live in a society that is increasingly asymmetrical and idiosyncratic, focused on the sites of our desire – as such they are supremely authentic, however bizarre or even unmentionable they may be. Could the authenticity of a desire ever be denied? Authenticity thus proves to be rather dangerous, in this case almost ridiculous, an undeniable tautology.[23] Moreover, precisely on this uncertain terrain the subject realizes one of Rousseau's dreams: What one feels *really is*. It is finally authentic. This is the case, however, in a paradoxical way, namely, by cultivating what is not equal (for example, luxury). The subject is no longer what it is, if it ever was; it is instead what it desires and possesses. Authenticity, in other terms, is regulated by the market. One need only think – as was noted above – of competing phenomena like luxury goods and tattooing, outcomes reinforced by the crises of the most recent decades. In both cases we are dealing with the emergence of idiosyncratic subjects who only want to be themselves at any cost and, in all respects, incomparable. Authenticity, like a leitmotiv and guiding value, has taken the place of Christian (as well as democratic and Enlightenment) equality. In this framework, no ideality is able to resist: The ideal and transcendent symbols of a universal humanity vanish and make room for a variegated and idiosyncratic humanity that wears its own symbols or even embodies them, depriving them of any transcendent significance. Just like those kids who, in the heat of the summer, wear t-shirts bearing the words from *Thus Spoke Zarathustra*: "You must have chaos within to give birth to a dancing star."

If one were to provide an ontology of populism, one would need to consider these articulations and their current modifications due to "aesthetic capitalism," a production that emphasizes the significance of the identity and self-recognition of the subject in its relative incomparability. This is a subject who is prone to aggression and exclusion with respect to others, who rediscovers itself in its own desires more than in its own needs, and who desires to be recognized as authentic and *true* reflections of the ego. This thrust leads back to moments and dreams of a past near and far, known or unknown, promises of a nostalgic feeling that imagines one's past as places inhabited by an inextinguishable nostalgia. The gaze turns to what is reassuring and casts upon the present a feeling that is uniformly melancholic. It is the age of *revival*, which technologically populates the present of its own past. Our age, studded with thousands of transient icons, which could be defined as an age of the naked, visible foundation that has taken the place of the invisible God and for that very reason is a foundation that is really quite flimsy. Its place and its *ubi consistam* are uncertain and perilous, enclosed within the desiring community that has replaced the ancient figure of the sovereign body.

2

The Aesthetization of Power

More on the "Withholding Power"

The Event of the New Testament

The history of the aestheticization of power is ancient and worth reconsidering from its very beginning, even if only to note that power contains, within the Christian world, a powerful and well-formed aesthetic character that already emerges in full clarity with the event of the New Testament. The theological-political vicissitudes of power in Christianity contain and express a double and contradictory spirit which remains consistent throughout its entire history: The messianic spirit and the historical-secular spirit of Christianity battle each other to the end. The realization of the idea of a *civitas christiana* requires the use of the representations, figures, and symbolic objectifications that universalize this power and make it palpable. Sovereign power itself is originarily legitimated by means of aesthetic modalities.

Proceeding in order, it makes sense to begin the discussion with the famous passage from Chapter 5 of the Gospel of Matthew that follows the Beatitudes in the Catholic tradition and the Sermon on the Mount in the reformed one. In a verse that embodies Jesus's *lectio humilis* while also containing an undeniable political inflection, Jesus says: You are the light of the world. A city on a hill cannot remain hidden (Matt. 5:14).

The messianic and political-messianic significance of this text is very clear. The humanity present here is already one to come, the intense symbol of the *civitas nova* that will both be and also not be of this earth. The messianic *civitas* is of this earth because Jesus Christ is the Lord of this world and must still consolidate, through the second coming, his lordship. Within this interrupted time, which becomes an anxious and ambiguous time marked by the presence-absence of the Lord, nothing less than history occurs. The disciples are already the redeemed people, and yet they still are not. It is difficult to say to which *civitas* they really belong: the present kingdom or the one yet to come. In either case, the image of the city on the hill as both the *exemplum* and the prefiguration of the kingdom to come resonates powerfully in the tradition of painting. The depiction of the city on the hill can be found in the Renaissance tradition from Mantegna to Cima da Conegliano to Bellini, as the *imago* of the *civitas* and of the kingdom to come that already reflects its light in the present. It thus constitutes a fundamental passage of the Christian imaginary that never stops looking for its figurative confirmation.

Before long, in Paul's Second Letter to the Thessalonians (thus always within the context of the New Testament), the light of the world seems to yield before the danger of the false prophets, of those who want to take the place of the one true Messiah:[1]

> As to the coming of our Lord Jesus Christ and our being gathered together to him, we beg you, brothers and sisters, (2) not to be quickly shaken in mind or alarmed, either by spirit or by word or by letter, as though from us, to the effect that the day of the Lord is already here. (3) Let no one deceive you in any way; for that day will not come unless the rebellion comes first and the lawless one is revealed, the one destined for destruction. (4) He opposes and exalts himself above every so-called god or object of worship, so that he takes his seat in the temple of God, declaring himself to be God. (5) Do you not remember that I told you these things when I was still with you? (6) And you know what is now restraining him, so that he may be revealed

> when his time comes. (7) For the mystery of lawlessness is already at work, but only until the one who now restrains it is removed. (8) And then the lawless one will be revealed, whom the Lord Jesus will destroy with the breath of his mouth, annihilating him by the manifestation of his coming. (9) The coming of the lawless one is apparent in the working of Satan, who uses all power, signs, lying wonders, (10) and every kind of wicked deception for those who are perishing, because they refused to love the truth and so be saved. (11) For this reason God sends them a powerful delusion, leading them to believe what is false, (12) so that all who have not believed the truth but took pleasure in unrighteousness will be condemned (2 Thessalonians 2:1–12).[2]

The light is blurring. False prophets and imposters want to establish an illegitimate kingdom and give credit to a false lord in the place of the true one. Thus, a sort of dialectic of the denied and betrayed archetype is established; the principle of the exercise of power in the form of representation is erased by the lookalike, who takes the place of the Lord by pretending to be him. This is the secret of the *mysterium iniquitatis*, of the Antichrist endowed with the finite/infinite power of the *pseudos*, of the one who seeks legitimacy by trying to be recognized as the true Lord, and thus by exhibiting tangible and shared signs (albeit counterfeits) of its own legitimacy. They are characters who deceive others, but also themselves, as the Second Letter of Peter also attests (see 2 Peter 2).

Right away, therefore, or almost, the messianic kingdom is threatened by deceitful figures, icons of a misleading appearance who try to muddy the waters and seize a power that is not rightfully theirs (see 2 Peter 3). Between the light of the foundation and its earthly reverberation there is a diaphragm that interrupts the trinitarian economy. This incident, inexplicable at first, produces a dramatic break in the relation between heaven and earth, and works its way into its heavenly descendants and their hypostases. It is as if the relation between the Father and the Son no longer functioned in any of its articulations and allowed a third to enter into the game surreptitiously by pretending to play a critical role while it was in fact dismantling it. This announces, already in the context of the New Testament, albeit in an implicit way, the Schmittian idea of the "state of exception." It is therefore a matter of understanding why the radiant light of the kingdom is not sufficient, why the horizon that ought to be intensely illuminated is unexpectedly darkened, producing a disorientation and a confusion that is nourished by the lack of the Lord's coming. In the eyes of the Lord, a thousand years are like a day, according to the Second Letter of Peter (2 Peter 2, 8), which recalls Paul's admonitions to justify the discomfort of God's eagerly waiting people.

On the one side we are dealing with the vivid light, like a lamp that shines in the darkness (2 Peter 1), to invoke another evangelical metaphor of the disciples who become *imago regni*; on the other side there is the menacing face of the *mysterium iniquitatis*, which slows and obstructs the coveted realization of the kingdom. A rather dark picture takes shape – that of the glowing manifestation of evil in all forms of deceit and seductive wonders. The *mysterium iniquitatis* replaces the messianic kingdom of heaven with the diabolical face of the Antichrist, of the imposter, of he who is not Christ but presents himself as if he were: Here a primary aesthetic characteristic appears, that of *imitatio*. The Antichrist seduces by using his charms and trying to impose himself without a real claim to legitimacy. Reliant on deceptions to establish his supremacy, the aesthetic traits of this figure are obvious from the beginning.

The modern anti-utopia, the reversal of the meaning of the true end into the unredeemed end of all things, already looms as an increasingly impending nightmare. It was already announced from a great distance, in the oscillations of the texts of the New Testament. This would seem to allude to the fact that the Christian roots of modernity, as Hegel proposes,[3] have unfolded as a destiny since their inception. The admixture of the two moments (rather distinct in an earlier time) – the messianic end as *Vollendung*, as fulfillment, and the end as destruction or self-destruction – was already catching on. Slowly – and this is the point – the messianic motif comes to be understood in an increasingly negative way, all the way to Carl Schmitt, who in reality was not thinking about the second parousia of Christ, but instead about the Soviet revolution as the nihilistic chaos which must be stopped. For these reasons the "withholding power," the *katechon*, finally reappears in its actuality.

The waiting for annihilation that heralds the happy or unhappy end therefore bears within itself the need to turn the final moment into a spectacle that marks its importance and finality. At this moment, how could we not remember the exemplary conclusion of *Apocalypse Now*, the final words of Kurtz/Marlon Brando: "The horror, the horror …," which seems to validate the fear that time could indeed come to an end, its absolute implosion. Obviously, this position is not logical and reflects the obsession of an expectation lacking its own objects, of an empty time infiltrated by the ghosts of the imaginary: a time that is separated from life and therefore travels directly toward its own end, encountering no resistance along its itinerary. A time that has evacuated the living and its forms, leaving them behind; a time that exploits every event to reach the end of its course. The end almost becomes an obsession. What is announced is the end of time, almost as if time and the forms of the living were caught up in an irreconcilable conflict and able to remain there forever, condemned for eternity as happens in the works of Anselm Kiefer.

With this in mind, it is difficult to conceive how historical time belongs to life: the time which runs through it – through genesis, maturation, and death – and a time of life in its fullest form rather than time that is bloodless and anxious about the end. Historical time ignores the possibility that exists beyond the limits of historical temporality, beyond messianic time, that introduces us to an evolutionary dimension of temporality: a conception that does not link time to genesis in itself, to the inaugural instant and to that of its eventual destruction, but instead to its morphological growth, to an intensive-extensive dimension of growth-maturation. This time contains the event as a son, which carries its own fulfillment and thus does not project beyond itself, to a time of expectation, to an event that comes from beyond (as happens in the case of historical time, the younger sibling of messianic time). The temporality that places the idea of morphogenesis – said here in passing – at its centre, threatens to reform the time that carries us back to the origins. This temporality is a time of nature, but also the *nature of time*, which radically transforms the axes of empty time. By immersing us back into the time of life, even the meaning of the middle time is transformed, of that purely "historical" time which we will discuss in the following pages.

To pick up the thread of our discussion: Empty time, which needs to be refilled, is the time of the *katechon*, and the withholding power, or better, the power that delays before the unavoidable abyss, is modelled on it. It is not surprising that the *katechon* has resurfaced in philosophical discussion during a time of political crisis like ours, almost as if it were now the very symbol of this crisis.[4] For this it will be necessary, in the pages that follow, to traverse the history of the *katechon* in order to assess the profound and truly inescapable significance of its solemn advance – to explain in a secular key the meaning of Paul's words: the crisis of the *katechon*, the crisis of the withholding power, the melancholy experienced when we accept that this is our time. Therefore, we will follow the traces of its history in the framework of a journey that, from its first steps, allows our time to transpire. It is a process in which the messianic finality of the originary appropriation of the kingdom ("you are the light of the world") is slowly replaced by the political systemization of the kingdom itself. This event reveals the distant origins of that catastrophic destiny pressuring the contemporary imaginary, that only seemingly very recent and unforeseen implosion that made us speak of nonexistent objects like "the end of history" and "the society of the spectacle," entertaining theses basically akin to authors of different, if not opposing, politics like Francis Fukuyama and Guy Debord.

The Return of the *Katechon* and the Legitimacy of Our Time

The Pauline metaphor of the *katechon*, or of the "withholding power," of the ring that manages to gather what escapes, is nonetheless struck by a truly surprising actuality, by a world filled with rancor and nostalgia for a time that once was – a world frightened by a present overrun with nationalisms and with localisms that are almost vernacular, and which has lost sight of traditional forms of legitimacy. The demand for identity – to know who we are, where we come from, and the nature of our access to the world – becomes increasingly intense. The theme of "the legitimacy of the modern age," to refer to the title of a famous book by Hans Blumenberg, is by no means unusual, but roots itself in a distant time.[5] This will be absolutely decisive for every prognosis about our time, as we affix our gaze upon the present.

Moreover, by now we know all too well who we are, as if we were no longer unconscious. Today has crossed thousands of identities through the most diverse media and guises, confusing one with the other. We are too much, and too many. But our time seems at the same time to want to lessen this excess of mediated awareness, almost producing a confounding abyss. Furthermore, it comes as no surprise that we are dealing with – as has already been said – the great fear, nourished by modernity, of a time emptied out to the point of entropy, understood here in the broad sense as the tendency to lose energy. It is the fear of disintegration, the idea that historically, taking on different names over time, the ring does not close – that we are dealing with nihilism, total mobilization, the Anthropocene.[6] This suggests a very long and rather significant path to reach what is currently happening. On this, one need not be deceived by the immense temporal acceleration which consumes our time.[7] What we are considering here is not at all a completely unscripted panorama but has, instead, developed over the course of centuries.

In this sense nothing is more indicative of the difficulties, not to mention the real failure, of the process of the rationalization of the world on which Max Weber had trained his gaze.[8] Secularization, by wanting to establish a provisional equality between terms that were, after all, entirely semantically distinct, proceeds hesitantly and does not move directly from the sacred to the profane. This also, and perhaps above all, impacts the political sphere. Secularization has always had more difficulty promoting itself when it sets the sphere of the sacred completely aside. At least from this point of view, Carl Schmitt's claim that the political lexicon has a completely theological origin still retains all its strength.[9] This, as we will see, has much to do with the structure and the crisis of democracy.

To express the idea using a paradox, which is nevertheless very well founded, one might suspect that even the most hopefully secular legitimization of political power cannot but depend on a foundation that is not completely foreign to the sphere of the sacred. Moreover, the idea of a purely secular foundation of political power also seems to coincide with its deepest crisis.

It is in this framework that we should understand the increasingly intense interest in political theology in the context of Italian philosophy, beginning with the publication of Schmitt's *The Nomos of the Earth* in the 1950s. From Massimo Cacciari to Roberto Esposito and Giorgio Agamben, the reflection on the *katechon* develops in a framework where the exegesis of the New Testament issue proposed in Paul's Second Letter to the Thessalonians opens the pathway to the understanding and the self-understanding of our time in diverse and multiform ways.[10] We are therefore dealing with – and this has never been emphasized enough – a diagnosis of the modern *over the long term*. At stake is an exquisitely philosophical-political question with clear aesthetic implications (not surprisingly, it has not aroused much interest in the theological and historical-religious realm: for example, the *Index Patristicus* has no entry for the term "*katechon*"). The aesthetic slant of the question is above all connected to what Marie-José Mondzain and Giorgio

Agamben have defined as the "trinitarian economy." This is the idea that the structure of worldly power follows the trinitarian design, for which – as we will see in the following pages – the figure of the Father has an epiphany in the sovereign, analogous to but inferior in rank to the Son. Here the system of representation and self-representation comes into play. This aesthetic (and also aestheticist) aspect is moreover connected to the very idea of the *katechon*, as the form that withholds and restrains.

What is defined as the trinitarian economy refers to a monarchical dimension of power. It moves from principle to principle and forbids the duplication of principles. To outline a question that extends over centuries – an invisible hypostasis is expected to grant access to a visible formalization of power. This latter is nevertheless ersatz and, in some way, certified by the fact that the structure of the visible, or better, its legitimization, is valid only because it derives from a semi-invisible principle, or at least only secondarily visible through its own hypostasis. In this key, the aesthetic moment becomes intrinsic to the very structuring of power in the course of an event that runs through Greek and Latin patristics from Hippolytus to Tertullian to Gregory of Nazianzus. Legitimate power and the legitimization itself of power depend on this aesthetic dimension, which is semi-epiphanic in nature. It is a dynamic structure that recalls "the economy of mystery" and with it "the mystery of the economy,"[11] where the reverberation of this entire process is intensely terrestrial. On the other hand, we are dealing with a transfer of energies that establish a sort of new Christian cosmicity, retracing it and modifying the Greek one: One thinks of the metaphor of the ring, which refers to an energetic organization in which there are no moments of fracture or loss of energy. From the interruption of this perfect economy there results an energetic devaluation that shares a great many features with nihilism.

This economy makes it possible for a reconciliation in which the transcendent God can take charge of the world and accommodate both the normal state and the state of exception.[12] It is an aesthetic structure, one of epiphanic reverberation, which stabilizes a link between heaven and earth, configuring itself as the *conditio sine qua non* of the establishment of the political order. As we will see more clearly later, this is a plastic order open both in terms of history and in terms of vision, without the two ever separating. The scanning of the hypostases makes it possible to gaze upon the historical event, which is profiled in its mobile quality insofar as it is included in the trinitarian movement. The apex of this event is represented by Bisanzio with Constantine the Great and his theologian Eusebius of Caesarea. The important step that leads us beyond these parallel theses from Marie-José Mondzain and Giorgio Agamben on the trinitarian economy regards the order of vision that is connected to it. This is an element that will become central to the course of the argument that will be developed here.

According to Hans Belting, the idea of the trinity suggests that reality is organized tri-dimensionally, "opening" the space of vision and emphasizing its quality of depth.[13] This allows it – I would add – to temporalize space and to understand it as a pathway, as a journey with a destination. It is a thesis that can be formulated with and beyond Belting as regards the birth of perspective in the Western world. Belting seems to be saying that it is the space of vision that constitutes the presupposition behind the very possibility of historical unfolding, as the developing of a history. Perspective places progress at its very core, the idea of a journey in the direction of the horizon understood as the completion and conclusion of the course. The fundamental presupposition of history is therefore established in the structures of vision prior to its properly political ones. In order to extend the argument and anticipate its consequences, one would be right to say that the trinitarian economy – in reference to the lexicon of Mondzain/Agamben – also makes historical development possible due to the very fact that it proposes a perspective and establishes depth by avoiding a rigid monotheism akin to Islam.

With perspective, one is also open to pluralism, which makes a view of the world (in the literal and metaphorical sense) possible. The centre is divided on two lines like the focus of a gaze, prefiguring a journey both real and illusory, connected to the condition of the point of view, and thus to the appearance and the transience of human existence. But precisely by virtue of this transience, to take up Belting again, there is progress. Time becomes, in this framework, a product and a result of the visual horizon. The horizon of worldly appearance is secured, in its secondary nature with respect to the end, by the fact of being supported by a final outcome that initiates it and in which the entire process must be resolved. In this way a symbolic schema is established that extends up to the beginnings of modernity, a schema that lives by a visible/invisible archetype that radiates in time. But the economy, as with every economic structure, could also go into crisis. In other words, the relation among the three hypostases could at a certain point be interrupted. The *elì elì lemà sabactàni* (the "Oh God, oh God why have you forsaken me?" that Jesus screams at the height of the passion), or the crisis of the archetype and its darkening, is a possibility. It is this image, however, which establishes the modern world and has difficulty rediscovering the celestial light. The crisis of the structure of the archetype nonetheless produces the darkening of its capacity to make sense of the world and creation: In the absence of the light of the other, the earth and its events become obscure and difficult to read. On the other side, the light of the archetype is extinguished when its manifestation fails. The archetype blinds itself: If it is not seen, it cannot see.[14]

On the other hand, the *katechon*, as Massimo Cacciari has shown, includes in itself an intrinsically mythopoietic and inventive value, where it makes its form available to situations in which it can exercise its force.[15] Another aesthetic determination becomes central in this scope which calls us back – by conceptual analogy – to the tradition of German classicism. Here we meet the most intimate core of the aesthetic-political relation, which I will outline in the following pages. It emerges in Winckelmann's famous comment about the statue of Laocoön: No definition of beauty is, upon closer inspection, as *katechonic* as this.[16] The figure of Laocoön, which stands with "noble simplicity" and "silent grandeur," seems to present itself as the ideal continuation of kingly power, like that depicted on the famous cover of Hobbes's *Leviathan*. Even in this case a body contains heterogeneous elements and must lead them to a dynamic unity. Laocoön is compared to a sea crossed by deep and restless currents, which do not rise to its otherwise calm and peaceful surface: "The last and most eminent characteristic of the Greek works is a noble simplicity and sedate grandeur in gesture and expression. As the bottom of the sea lies peaceful beneath a foaming surface, a great soul lies sedate beneath the strife of passions in Greek figures. It is in the face of Laocoön [that] this soul shines with full lustre, not confined however to the face, amidst the most violent sufferings."[17]

This passage proposes, with great clarity, the relation between strength and form; a purely political relation, of a qualitative nature, in which the form arrives and completely expresses its own potentiality by silencing chaos and anomie. In the decades that precede and immediately follow the French Revolution, aesthetic and political forms are closely related in German culture, almost as if one were the model for the other. The description of Laocoön announces the model of an agnostic form, a model that is both aesthetic and political.[18] It proposes, on this basis, the need for a dynamic form that can contain contrasting jolts and energies thanks to its plastic and resilient nature. Furthermore, it recognizes the need for a form that introjects time, the principle of disintegration and transience, converting it into a factor of morphogenesis.

The centrifugal forces no longer oppose the solidity of the formal structure, but instead build it up. The form expresses the capacity to contain the multiple, to keep, to introject, and even to take advantage of the tensions that pervade it without slipping into anomie. The idea emerges, almost implicitly, that this could have been and must be the political and aesthetic-political form capable of resisting the winds of the Revolution. In this framework, history rejoins nature and intersects with it; the power that was threatened is granted a historical dimension along with a natural one, in both a particular and broad sense, in that it derives its legitimacy from a divine sanction. This is a fundamental transition that will have a development of equal importance in the *Frühromantik* and particularly in the early thought of Friedrich Schlegel, who in the course of working out the form of the novel defines it as a dynamic and transformational form, capable of carrying within it a multiplicity of unrelated things, always on the verge of anomie and of absolute particularization.[19] Precisely this infinite particularization of the social structure constitutes the aesthetic and political risk of modernity.

It was necessary to anticipate these aspects before returning to the historical course we are following because here is the true inception of the issue, the point (or at least one of the points) from which Carl Schmitt began to advance the idea of the withholding power in relation to modern anomie, of which Protestantism and Romanticism would be the symbols (the one, dominated by the principle of *Affekt*, as the metaphor of immediate feeling, and the other as the example of extreme occasionalism, of extreme fragmentation).[20] We are dealing with a misrepresentation of self-awareness achieved by the *Frühromantik*, dictated perhaps by a not-so-innocent point of view, namely, one aimed at political romanticism. Precisely in light of this Romantic form, it is worth taking another look at the issue, now with an eye toward the past. In fragment 116 of *Athenaeum* Schlegel claims:

> Romantic poetry is a progressive, universal poetry. Its aim isn't merely to reunite all the separate species of poetry and put poetry in touch with philosophy and rhetoric. It tries to and should mix and fuse poetry and prose, inspiration and criticism, the poetry of art and the poetry of nature; and make poetry lively and sociable, and life and society poetical; poeticize wit and fill and saturate the forms of art with every kind of good, solid matter for instruction, and animate them with the pulsations of humor …. It alone can become, like the epic, a mirror of the whole circumambient world, an image of the age. And it can also – more than any other form – hover at the midpoint between the portrayed and

> the portrayer, free of all real and ideal self-interest, on the wings of poetic reflection, and can raise that reflection again and again to a higher power, can multiply it in an endless succession of mirrors. It is capable of the highest and most variegated refinement, not only from within outwards, but also from without inwards; capable in that it organizes – for everything that seeks a wholeness in its effects – the parts along similar lines, so that it opens up a perspective upon an infinitely increasing classicism.[21]

The Romantic form opposes anomie by introjecting it and making it the motor of its being. Thus, it also advances a meta-reflection on morphogenesis, proposing the dynamic form as the only one suited to modernity and its temporal acceleration.[22]

Anomie, in this truly aesthetic-political framework, is nothing if not a loss of the formal structure that leaves multiplicity untethered in its naked singularity. Due to the centrifugal movement, the particulars tend to become increasingly minute and minimal, to the point of reaching that *mysterium consumptionis*, the Romantic ineffable – which, as Hegel said, borders on the non-existent. Romantic poetry represents a plastic form that is also an aesthetic and political model for containing the chaos of the epoch, once again making the many into one. One faces a time of great duration, an age – as Nietzsche states in the third *Untimely Meditation* – of "atomistic revolution."[23] Artistic form and aestheticization in this case exchange their features. On the other hand, it is precisely on the aesthetic level that the fundamental distinction between legitimacy and legality, developed in the polemic dialogue between Schmitt and Blumenberg, comes to be defined.[24] Leaving aside these anticipatory remarks, it is time to deal with the historical precedents of the theological-political issue that is at the centre of these reflections, that of the *katechon*, of the withholding power. If we do not, everything will remain quite obscure.

3

The *Katechon* Between the Ancient and the Modern

From Epiphany to Prestige

Paul and the Second Letter to the Thessalonians

The question of the *katechon* has important precedents in ancient philosophy and in the Old Testament, but it achieves its full importance – as has already been said – in Paul's Second Letter to the Thessalonians (2 Thessalonians 2:1–12, in particular 6–7), where he claims that the event of the Antichrist is underway, but that it will encounter the resistance of the *katechon*, that is, its "withholding power."[1] This power performs a role that is both positive and negative: On the one hand, it blocks the arrival of the Antichrist, and, thus, of a radical evil; on the other hand, this also blocks the new parousia of Christ, who should destroy the adversary when and if he reveals himself. The future destiny of the *katechon* is connected to this ambiguity, a path on which the negative valence of the concept increasingly gives way to positive interpretations.[2] Paul appeals to Old Testament sources that tend to accentuate the negative face of the *katechon*, understood as that which slows down the coming of the Messiah (even today, it is worth remembering that the religious parties in Israel accuse the secular ones of building a *katechon* against the coming of the Messiah). The question is rather delicate, given that on one side it refers to the affirmation of the one legitimate power, the Kingdom of God, announced with the coming of Christ that reaffirms his lordship over the world. Every other kingdom or power, in this light, turns out to be either illegitimate or takes on a secondary significance in relation to the first.

The Antichrist presents himself in charming and alluring forms. He does not deny Christ's legitimacy, and, in fact, he affirms it by taking his place. If one reads Paul's letter through a contemporary lens, the Antichrist takes on features that are undeniably aestheticizing, referring to multiple aesthetic themes. In particular

- an *aesthetics of prestige*, which takes its authority from the aura of the one it simulates and would like to replace;
- the theme of the *double*, of the *lookalike*, or, to refer to Freud, of the *doppelgänger*, as it appears in a duplicating form;
- the concept of *kitsch*, as it plays with the status of authenticity.

The Antichrist almost seems to prefigure the features of aesthetic capitalism which were mentioned above: in fact, when he seeks legitimacy through capricious, charming, and deceitful actions, he does so because he aims to feed his own ego and legitimate his exaggerated claims. This is the real added value connected to a sovereign position acquired through illicit ways and forms.[3] The Antichrist wields a seductive power, like that of a charismatic leader. In the modern age this assumes, among others, the Marxian semblance of ideology, of an appearance that wants to be certified as true and in possession of power.

Paul's warning is crystal clear: He alerts the Thessalonians so that they are not tricked by someone who takes advantage of the fact that the day of the Lord's return is near (2 Thessalonians 1–2). The Antichrist thus reveals himself to be an illegitimate substitute, as the imposter, the one who replaces the true Lord by imitating his features and way of being. Once again, through the mimetic theme, an aesthetic determination related to politics emerges. Thus, we could say that the double/Antichrist anticipates kitsch as the inauthentic that wishes to pass itself off as the authentic even though it is obviously a counterfeit. Similar to certain examples of kitsch, the Antichrist transforms and domesticates the sacred, making it familiar and less numinous.[4] In this framework, the possibility of a diarchy is not expected: Only *one* can be the legitimate sovereign.[5] This is one of the central points that accompanies the story of legitimacy and legitimization, which includes the arbitrary aestheticization of power attempted today by charismatic figures who grant themselves prestige without possessing the necessary imprimatur. Let us propose, starting from here – and to anticipate the question in all its complexity – an aesthetics of legitimate power which acts as a counterpoint to the aestheticization of illegitimate power.

For its part, the aesthetics of legitimate power presents itself as an epiphanic aesthetics, which will be articulated in all of its strength by Eusebius of Caesarea in his *Oration in Praise of the Emperor Constantine*, where he considers the need for a worldly monarchy and a divine monarchy. The two monarchies represent realms which are not overlapping, but interdependent, organized according to a system of emanations that move from the superior principle to the inferior one, which in this framework nevertheless maintains its autonomy. A complex symmetry is established between one level and the other that gives order in the relations between heaven and earth.

Let us now return to the passage from Paul, where he announces the coming of the "man of iniquity":

> Never let anyone deceive you in this way. It cannot happen until the Great Revolt has taken place and the Rebel, the Lost One, has appeared. This is the Enemy, the one who claims to be so much greater than all that men call "god," so much greater than anything that is worshiped, that he enthrones himself in God's sanctuary and claims that he is God. [...] Rebellion is at its work already, but in secret, and the one who is holding it back has first to be removed before the Rebel appears openly. The Lord will kill him with the breath of his mouth and will annihilate him

> with his glorious appearance at his coming. But when the Rebel comes, Satan will set to work: there will be all kinds of miracles and a deceptive show of signs and portents, and everything evil that can deceive those who are bound for destruction because they would not grasp the love of the truth which could have saved them. The reason why God is sending a power to delude them and make them believe what is untrue is to condemn all who refused to believe in the truth and chose wickedness instead (2 Thessalonians 3–4).[6]

The identification of the "man of wickedness" who becomes the Antichrist (and we will refer to him in these terms from now on) and of the *katechon*, of the withholding power, will propose an almost infinite sequence of interpretations whose significance for the definition, articulation, and legitimization of worldly (in relation to heavenly) power cannot easily be underestimated in the history of Christianity. This almost endless sequence of positions with respect to the Pauline text stretches from Jerome to Crisostomo and Tertullian, developing further (not without significant interruptions) with Constantine I and Eusebius of Caesarea, and on to the Reformation, to Luther and Calvin, and further on to the Russian thinkers, from Rozanov to Sestov, finally reaching its culmination in the epic encounter between Carl Schmitt and Jacob Taubes, in whose background looms the captivating and ultimately victorious shadow of Walter Benjamin.

What is at stake in this vast trans-millennial story? First and foremost, the characteristics and definition of the kingdom to come, along with those of its enemies, are interrogated. The church and the empire are called into question as principal actors in this affair, the institutions of modern power that throughout the course of this event debate and validate their legitimacy. In the face of an early and intense push to subvert the Roman Empire, which characterized the movement of the zealots during the time of Jesus (and in which Jesus himself was involved through John the Baptist, who belonged to the movement), we slowly see a re-evaluation of the imperial structure.[7] Over the course of the long itinerary that we will trace through its principal stages, we will also outline the characteristics of illegitimate power, which are simultaneously an ideology of power and an ideological power that takes on seductive and deceptive guises. In the case of the zealots, these might also be common everyday features, such as Herod's way of dressing "alla Romana" (Roman style), seen as a caricature by his fellow citizens and subjects, the sign of an almost laughable submission to Roman power, intended to acquire prestige and recognition in the eyes of the conquerors.

As we now arrive at the mechanisms that drive the process, we can say that the *katechon* inaugurates the political space, and more precisely, the space of a politics founded on principles of legitimacy. The *katechon* does this by slowing the messianic process, the journey of history to salvation, and by making possible the conception and the necessity of a middle time and ground that comes before the definitive affirmation of the kingdom. While carrying out a negative role with respect to the parousia of Christ,[8] the *katechon* aids in the development and completion of the messianic event. Moreover: It explains the inexplicable delay of the second coming of Christ. The catechonic limit even comes to be viewed with melancholy as soon as it fails.

Tertullian and Augustine

It is in this framework that the rereading of the question of the *katechon* in the Latin context becomes central, for example, in a second-century author like Irenaeus. Here it is revealed that the *mysterium iniquitatis*, which the apostle Paul mentions in his Second Letter to the Thessalonians, is none other than a figure of the *pseudos*, of the double, of the lookalike imposter. The negative meaning of the *pseudos*, of the power of the Antichrist, the very representative of the illegitimate double, appears in its full importance. As E.T.A. Hoffmann teaches in *The Sandman*, the double attracts and repels at the same time, producing an effect of infinite fascination due to its intense aesthetic connotations. The Antichrist, according to Irenaeus, "sets aside idols to persuade [men] that he himself is God, raising up himself as the only idol, having in himself the multifarious errors of the other idols. This he does, in order that they who do [now] worship the devil by means of many abominations, may serve himself by this one idol."[9] The Antichrist is therefore the doppelgänger, the lookalike par excellence, the "wicked judge" in which earthly Jerusalem takes refuge, the widow who seeks shelter "to be avenged of her adversary, Which also he shall do in the name of his kingdom: he shall remove his kingdom into that [city], and shall sit in the temple of God, leading astray those who worship him, as if he were Christ."[10]

In this context a problem of the highest order emerges, which more precisely reveals how much and what the Pauline interpretation of the "man of wickedness" signifies as the one who produces seductions and charms. The first and most important seduction is that the Antichrist is not the Messiah, the one who comes, but – as Bruno Latour says – un *dieu factice*, a "factish god" and, thus, an inauthentic one insofar as God makes and creates and is himself not created; in particular, in our case, he does not create himself by presenting himself as an idol.[11]

In some sense this proposes – by taking leave of the theological metaphor – the primacy of the artifice over the artifact, which can exist legitimately only in a symmetrical relation of dependence on that same artifice. If the artifact denies its origins, it becomes an idol, a double that does not want to be recognized as such, a figure of aesthetic semblance, which is already the principle of aestheticization. As Latour reveals, this is not at all universal, since in some examples from African culture, for example, it is possible to "make God," inverting the trajectory that runs from creator to created. The idol would therefore be derived from an inversion of the second with the first, of the made with the maker, and thus become the principle of a perturbation of the "divine economy" and an aspect of the false aesthetic appearance.

The Antichrist therefore represents the idolatrous faith, the imposition of the false *eidolon*, of a false appearance that takes the place of the true Messiah, the one and true Lord of this world. The Antichrist is the hypostasis that has lost contact with the archetype. In it the interruption of the exchange between the immanent horizon and the transcendent one is announced and established, which guarantees the structural integrity of political power, its balanced economy of representation. The divine economy claims the primacy of the transcendent horizon over the first, and not the opposite, which would bring about the fictitious double and thus to an economy of the inauthentic, of trickery, of the tendentially plebian double, a intrinsically kitsch camouflage which replaces the authentic and unique, and thus completely irreplaceable principle. Not surprisingly, Irenaeus, in *Against Heresies*, refers to the prophet Daniel (Dan. 17) where the angel who flew toward the dawn and fell is called into question, not finding in his elevation a counterpart in the archetype. The Antichrist and his deceptions will therefore be exorcized by knowing his number (666), which keeps us from being deceived and falling under the spells of the evil one.[12] Naturally, even the identification of the Antichrist is cryptic, as is his figure, since the number refering to the name is nonetheless unknowable and unpronounceable due to the peculiarity of the Saviour's adversary.[13] As Tyconius (the Greek writer from the fourth century engaged in the anti-Donatist controversy) will show us, the Antichrist can worm his way into the very body of the church, constituting its impure part by becoming a disturbing and confusing element and thus a new pseudos.[14] And yet, the bipartition of the church coincides, on the other hand, with an elaboration of the Pauline teaching according to which the church is the body of Christ.

The idea of the *katechon*, at least initially, carries a negative connotation. It can be understood, as happens in Jerome, as the empire which obstructs the new coming, or (in Irenaeus and Tyconius) as the dark part of the church and its body that corresponds to the bipartition in the very body of the Lord already announced by Paul. The possibility of a positive take on the *katechon* develops on two parallel levels, in the Latin patristics of the third century, with Tertullian and Augustine, and in the Greek ones with Eusebius of Caesarea and Nicephorus. The question can be articulated on two levels that run parallel to each other. On the one side, in the Latin patristics one finds a revaluation of the imperial structure that is, in a manner of speaking, unpacked and separated from its original political-religious context. This is what the history of the concept, through Augustine and Tertullian, shows us. On the other side, in the context of the Greek patristics, it deals with a legitimization of imperial power, which grounds imperial power in a juridical-theological key by reinforcing its fragile juridical foundations.

It was Augustine, through the duplication of the kingdoms and of the divine and human cities, who granted to Rome a central importance however limited to the political sphere. Thanks to this definition of the provinces of the two kingdoms, at once rigid and functional, Augustine infinitely reduced the intensity of the conflict between the kingdoms hidden behind the question of the *katechon*. In *Apologeticum*, Tertullian instead recognizes in the empire a real impediment – precisely a *katechon* – which blocks the final dissolution, the end of the world, which would thus arrive as a negative event and by no means be greeted as the long-awaited messianic event. The institution of the empire and its stability are – according to Augustine – a protection for everyone, and the empire is a political form that does not identify itself with Roman society and its vices.[15] The empire thus arises as a form of universal power, taking on characteristics that Dante Alighieri recognized in *De Monarchia*.

But why is the empire liberated from pagan religion and not suppressed by it? Both Augustine and Tertullian employ a rationalistic, almost proto-Enlightenment, argument that suggests pagan religion is in itself irrational and contrary to the finality of the empire. On the one hand, paganism suffers from immorality, which makes the empire-form "unpresentable" on the moral level, its legitimacy on the juridical-political level notwithstanding. The passages are, regarding this matter, almost comical in their references: For example, Tertullian claims that Socrates and Cato offered their wives to their friends in an undoubtedly unseemly gesture.[16] On the other hand, the pagan religion falls short not only on the level of customs but also on, broadly speaking, the argumentative level: It provides explanations, such as in the case of natural processes, but they are so detailed and numerous in their meticulous correspondence between the individual phenomena and the deities that they appear as laughable as they are inefficient. The pagan gods are, on this basis, taken to be demons rather than true divinities.[17] Paradoxically, it is necessary to defend the empire and the emperor from themselves and from the threat of a false religion that would end up dragging the political structure connected to them into the whirlpool of its inevitable demise. Therefore, the Christians pray anxiously for the emperors. Tertullian attests: "Thither we Christians, looking up with hands spread open, because without guilt, with head uncovered, because we are not ashamed, finally without a prompter, because we pray from the heart; are ever praying for all kings, that they may have a long life, a secure dominion, a safe home, valiant armies, faithful senate, a righteous people, a world at peace, and whatever be the desire both of the man and of the king."[18]

Of course, by honouring Caesar – Tertullian clarifies – one honours a man and not God. Caesar will never be a god for the Christians as he was in the pagan world: As emperor, he is simply a man.[19] Upon closer inspection, treating this figure as an idol would invalidate his imperial power. Tertullian claims (by emphasizing a fundamental point that will be developed fully in Eusebius of Caesarea), however, that through the emperor divine power is conveyed and almost transfused. In this way a dialectic of image and representation is articulated: The legitimacy of imperial power derives precisely from the fact that it represents in an asymmetrical way, and not through direct reflection, a divine hypostasis. The emperor *matters* precisely because he is the hypostasis of God. And it is in this way that the Christianization of the empire begins, whose triumph Eusebius of Caesarea will celebrate in *The Oration in Praise of the Emperor Constantine*. Obviously, we are dealing with a movement that does not begin or move forward without resistance, as Giovanni Crisostomo, another author of this era, will show us shortly.

According to Tertullian, the emperor thus represents a barrier against chaos, against anomie, and a true *katechon*, in whom the term begins to take on a positive meaning. Here the "withholding" function becomes entirely dominant over the messianic purpose, for which the withholding power would only represent an intermediate term. The mystery of anomie is thus cleansed of every messianic trait, completely distanced from its originary significance; only the idea of resistance remains, while the one who pushes to become manifest, the redeeming Christ, tends to vanish. Tertullian writes: "We have also another and a greater need to pray for the Emperors, and moreover for the whole estate of the Empire, and the fortunes of Rome, knowing, as we do, that the mighty shock which hangeth over the whole worlds, and the end of time itself, threatening terrible and grievous things, is delayed because of the time allowed to the Roman Empire. We would not therefore experience these things, and while we pray that they may be put off, we favour the long continuance of Rome."[20]

The end of the world evoked in the second century amidst a climate of great and almost desperate waiting (as the apocalyptic literature attests),[21] is overturned in a completely negative and fateful event, such that the new parousia of Christ seems to be hidden behind a dread that translates the coveted anticipation for the end into terror. *The anti-utopia arises in this way, taking shape behind Christianity*, which had made the anticipation for the kingdom its central focus. Moreover, as we will see definitively and with full awareness in Dostoevsky, the Antichrist is foreshadowed as the ghost who validates the anti-utopian and at times totalitarian imaginary belonging to late modernity and its response to the urgent chaos, whether real or imagined.

These presuppositions radically modify the theological order, produce a division of kingdoms and of their precincts, and encourage them to draw out clear distinctions with insurmountable boundaries between the *civitas Dei* and *civitas homini*. This is the perspective which Augustine introduces in *De Civitate Dei*. The fourth book is of particular importance, where the exaltation of the empire is accompanied by the work of dismantling and the actual symbolic destruction of the pagan religion.[22] One could define this as the Christian Enlightenment, which disintegrates the temple of ancient religion, also due to its limited functionality. Trinitarian monotheism emerges as a superior model from the rational point of view, and therefore – one could say – from that of argumentative functionality (namely, in relation to its ability to explain natural and historical phenomena). For example, what is the use – as Augustine asserts critically – of proposing a god for each component of a plant's development – from the stem, to the leaves, to the corolla? This is an argumentative model that widely distributes causality and that can only be corrected by a logical-religious thinking that is more ordered, rational, and economical.

This strategy obviously serves to exalt Christianity. On this basis the empire itself acquires a functional significance: It avoids multiplying the hypostases, simplifies the hierarchies, and makes things more efficacious. According to Augustine, Christians would better secure the continuity of the empire: If the Romans "had ignored or despised the multitude of false gods and acknowledged and worshipped the One with sincere faith and virtue, they would have had a better kingdom here, whatever its extent. Also, whether they had a kingdom here or not, they would have received an eternal kingdom hereafter."[23] In this way one can further acknowledge that God has acted "politically" by favouring the growth of the empire. This aspect even justifies the superiority and the victory of the empire over the Jewish world. Augustine's conclusions are truly terrible:

> Thus it was also that the Jews, who put Christ to death, were most righteously handed over to the glory of the Romans. The New Testament clearly reveals what is veiled in the Old: that the one true God is to be worshipped not for the sake of those earthly and temporal goods which divine providence grants to good and evil men alike, but for the sake of eternal life and everlasting rewards, and the fellowship of the supernal City itself. And so it was that the Romans, who sought and gained earthly glory by their virtues, such as they were, conquered those who, in their great wickedness, slew and rejected the Giver of true glory and of the Eternal City.[24]

This recognition of the empire depends on the fact that we are dealing with a conception of Christianity as *civitas peregrina* on the way toward its proper transcendent destiny.[25] The Christian is a citizen of two worlds, and this – as was highlighted[26] – relativizes the significance of the "give to Caesar" recorded in the three synoptic gospels. The Christian, to use the expression of the evangelical theologian Friedrich Gogarten, lives "in between times," *zwischen den Zeiten*: There is no longer a radical choice, such as between the empire and the messianic kingdom. The two laws do not conflict because they operate on different levels. In sum, and paradoxically, the empire is saved by its detractors, who are not the Christians but precisely those who created them!

The *katechon* thus becomes a positive power and no longer a negative one. It no longer simply represents a necessary restraint, which is still inscribed on the level of salvation, on the second coming of the Messiah: now it is functional to the emergence of a new power, a Christian empire (or on the way to being Christianized). The political form thus gains autonomy from the historical context and acquires a significance that resists its mortality. The *civitas peregrina* uses this path to become something totally other. It is about to become the *civitas christiana*, stable and no longer peregrina, which inaugurates a new era with Constantine. The divine empire becomes a universal political form, a model of political power, a markedly undying transcendental; from now on, finally stable, it will really be ready to endure over the course of millennia, and, at this point, almost forget the promised return of the Messiah that justifies – on the level of salvation – its stable/unstable presence in the course of the world. The "city on the hill" from Matthew 5, deprived of its utopian valence, nearly materializes in the end. Thanks to Christianity the empire is universalized, becomes the earthly equivalent of the kingdom of heaven, establishing with it a relation of epiphanic symmetry and correspondence which bestows a further aesthetic dimension upon the figure of the emperor. It is a symbolic formulation which consolidates and validates its full legitimacy, also producing the necessity for one of its reverberations on the figurative level.

Eusebius of Caesarea

The empire, or rather the emperor, stands in a relation of symmetry, imitation, and dependence with/on a superior structure, of which it constitutes a second and lateral epiphany. Eusebius of Caesarea (265–339) – to take a step back to the eastern patristics – confirms this. The trinitarian dialectic institutes an imitative pattern in this framework between the heavenly power and the terrestrial power, which repeats the relation between the Father and the Son. In this way the empire is no longer only a historical institution, but also an atemporal and eternal one. This transfer of universality – in the empire that becomes *civitas christiana* – makes every attack on it from now on a question of civilization, as witnessed by a long event which endures to the present. On this basis, moreover, a form of legitimization of political power will be defined, one based on an energy, on an economy of an *invisible that is made visible.*[27]

This type of legitimization of power places the empire on a higher level than the traditional one and normalizes the transmission of power on an etymologically and rigorously monarchical basis, which a priori excludes every form of diarchy. This fact transforms how the traditional legitimization of imperial power occurred in Roman times, when it descended from an arbitrary conjunction of the prerogatives of the *pontifex maximus* and the *praetor* in the figure of the emperor.[28] This is how it happened with Julius Caesar, who reunited these two offices by force, in his physical person, and then transferred them – through a transition as paradoxical as it is significant – to a son who is not natural but adopted, Augustus Caesar. This absolutely empirical and almost casual transition lacks any transcendental motive for political legitimization, which will be created only with Constantine and the idea of an organization of power founded mimetically, on the basis of the relation Father/Son, which will extend from the figures of imperial power to their reformulations. The relation, in the form of the imperial portrait, is here presented in an iconic sequence, within a transmission in images. The images therefore become necessary, suggesting an originary reproducibility of a power that spreads ever more extensively through its own icons.

It is on this foundation, as we will see below, that political power also functions in our time, by making recourse to an archetypical image that today becomes blurry almost to the point of disappearing.[29] In this context, the figure of Eusebius of Caesarea is absolutely central. His *The Life of The Blessed Emperor Constantine* articulates this in two texts: his oration on the thirtieth anniversary of his reign, and the royal discourse. Here it is established that the emperor rules over his subjects in a manner analogous to the relation between the Father and the Son, with the latter interpreting the kingdom of the Father *sub specie imperatoris*. Eusebius states:

> 4. He who is the pre-existent Word, the Preserver of all things, imparts to his disciples the seeds of true wisdom and salvation, and at once enlightens and gives them understanding in the knowledge of His Father's kingdom. Our emperor, His friend, acting as interpreter to the Word of God, aims at recalling the human race to the knowledge of God; proclaiming clearly in the ears of all, and declaring with powerful voice the laws of truth and godliness to all who dwell on the earth.

> 5. Once more, the universal Saviour expands the heavenly gates of His Father's kingdom to those whose course is thitherward from this world. Our emperor, emulous of His divine example, having purged his earthly dominion from every stain of impious error, invites each holy and pious worshipper within his imperial mansions, earnestly desiring to save with all its crew that mighty vessel of which he is the appointed pilot.[30]

On this basis a rigorously mono-archical power is structured that connects the worldly kingdom to the heavenly one. It can be affirmed only insofar as it is recognized in its irreplaceable uniqueness which does not permit equals or the proliferation of identical copies: Only on this basis can it extend and spread out over the entire universe as a metaphysical structure, according to a relation of affinity and similarity that is articulated mimetically, and thus in a key that could be defined as purely aesthetic. Eusebius writes:

> And surely monarchy far transcends every other constitution and form of government: for that democratic equality of power which is its opposite, may rather be described as anarchy and disorder. Hence there is one God, and not two, or three, or more: for to assert a plurality of gods is plainly to deny the being of God at all. There is one Sovereign; and His Word and royal Law is one: a Law not expressed in syllables and words, not written or engraved on tablets, and therefore subject to the ravages of time; but the living and self-subsisting Word, who Himself is God, and who administers His Father's kingdom on behalf of all who are after Him and subject to His power [...] and He Himself, who pervades all things, and is everywhere present, unfolding His Father's bounties to all with unsparing hand, has accorded a specimen of His sovereign power even to His rational creatures of this earth, in that He has provided the mind of man, who is formed after His own image, with divine faculties, whence

> it is capable of other virtues also, which flow from the same heavenly source. For He only is wise, who is the only God: He only is essentially good: He only is of mighty power, the Parent of justice, the Father of reason and wisdom, the Fountain of light and life, the Dispenser of truth and virtue: in a word, the Author of empire itself, and of all dominion and power.[31]

It thus becomes clear that the visible power is founded on an invisible power that precedes it and at the same time constitutes its hypostasis. In other terms, it is possible for the organization of power to share a form only insofar as its foundation is invisible – as Marie-José Mondzain has pointed out. Moreover, that makes it possible, paradoxically, that the diverse gazes only have one focus, which cannot be relativized as if we were dealing simply with one point of view; while, on the other hand, the visible figures of power are hypostases, transient figures of a more remote and profound demand that confirms them in their unstable temporal/eternal stability.

Later we will see how this model still carries weight in our present. The "trinitarian economy" depicted here grounds a model of political legitimization infinitely more grounded even with respect to that of the classical Roman Empire. It would be an error to understand this structure simply as a theocratic one. The sphere of the sacred organizes the worldly sphere in its various articulations that depend on the sacred but do not undergo its investiture; instead, they reveal a divine order that leaves, as such, room for the political and its decisions. It is a space in which human action is carried out and articulated – it is framed by the limits of a divine order but not directly sanctioned by it as would happen, instead, if the final hypostasis, if God himself, were the radiant shining down on the earth.

Thus we are dealing with a god, with a form of divinity, only partially invisible, which shows itself in its reflection. This gives rise to a sort of theological aesthetics that does not restrict the space of decision and, at least potentially, that of the legitimate plurality of gazes – a position guaranteed by the fact that the centre, even if it is not literally gone, nevertheless hides from view while still referring to itself. This is not relativism because the spectator is not imprisoned by its own point of view, insofar as the focus of the gaze is not oriented toward a visible object and therefore subjected to the laws of perspective, but toward the invisible that constitutes its ultimate and absolute presupposition. In other terms, in question is a partially invisible god, or rather, one visible only in its hypostases. We are therefore dealing with a particular pluralism, one belonging to a community that is founded on the invisible and that allows the foundation to reverberate in diverse forms and in diverse images. On the other hand, this schema, in its dynamic quality, makes room for history and events which are not – so to speak – "strangled" by theocratic domination. The trinity opens the space of historical time, and the Son truly belongs to this earth; therefore, the historical event holds all of its concreteness within a messianic history that reconnects the end with the beginning.

The journey through the Latin patristics is bumpier than the Greek one, where the preoccupation with the identification of the Antichrist seems to be right about the organization of power on theological grounds. Giovanni Crisostomo, in the *Comment on the Second Letter to the Thessalonians*, identifies the mysterium iniquitatis with Nero, interpreting the passage in Paul 2 Thessalonians 2 as a prudently cryptic invitation to rebellion against Rome in expectation of the coming of the Antichrist and the end of the waiting for the Messiah's return.[32] Behind the idea of the withholding power hides, according to Crisostomo, the Roman Empire, in so far as Paul predicts is dissolution. In Paul's eyes the Antichrist would be the emperor himself, who has ensconced himself as an evil within the imperial structure and carries out its dissolution. Christ himself will put an end to the anomie that unfolds from this movement, and his mere appearance will accomplish his own redemptive mission. Fundamentally, according to this reasoning, the withholding power dissolves by itself, leading to anomie and thus fostering the coming of the Messiah. Even if Crisostomo identifies the enemy in the Roman Empire, he, on the other hand, invites us not to succumb to messianic impatience (typical of early Christianity); ultimately, it is precisely the empire that plays a reassuring role in the context of a time where waiting has lost its anxious anticipation and in which one faces the need to protect and guarantee the normal course of daily life. Thus, in the fourth century, we witness how the issue of the *katechon* is settled in the context of Latin patristics, which increasingly pushes away the anxieties – or, as Taubes puts it, the "apocalyptic neuroses" – to make space for a church that immerses itself in the world and stands alongside imperial power without opposing it.

In the first phase of its history, the issue of the *katechon* contains within itself, more or less covertly, the conflict of kingdoms. The weight of the question is noteworthy since it regards what could be described as a celestial topology. Briefly: What it the space of the Kingdom of God? Or rather, what does the Saviour really save? Couldn't the Kingdom of God be located on the horizontal plane of a historical-messianic trajectory in which Jesus, the Christ, is confirmed as the true Lord of this earth, rather than on a vertical plane of transcendence? Couldn't the event of salvation happen in the here of history rather than in the sublime reaches of the heavens?[33] It is obvious that the first option has potentially contradictory consequences on the level of the legitimacy of the one or the other *imperium*. This is followed – if we accept a rather extreme hypothesis – a sort of *construction (or metaphysical constriction) of transcendence*. In other words, to hypothesize that transcendence, which in this instance could be defined as the vertical orientation of faith, deriving, at least in part, from the frustration over the delay in the second coming of Christ. This step, which is set up in Augustine, produces – as it were – a sort of dislocation of levels that gives the keys to the kingdom of heaven and the kingdom of earth and its government to different authorities.[34]

Transcendence and *its construction* allow for the definition of an order that tempers and integrates instances that were originarily opposed. The withholding power is now fully legitimated. The messianic vocation that once impeded the *katechon* is now diminished. It is a decisive transition, through which the *katechon* reverses its sign: It assumes, definitively, a positive meaning and nullifies its original one. The withholding power generates the *civitas christiana*, the announcement and almost sensible testimony of the kingdom to come. It is a process that has its ideal culmination, many centuries later, in Dante's *De Monarchia*, where the reconciling of these moments prefigures a perfect order:

> All of the arguments advanced so far are confirmed by a remarkable historical fact: namely the state of humanity which the Son of God either awaited, or himself chose to bring about, when he was on the point of becoming man for the salvation of mankind. For if we review the ages and the dispositions of men from the fall of our first parents (which was the turning point at which we went astray), we shall not find that there ever was peace throughout the world except under immortal Augustus, when a perfect monarchy existed. That mankind was then happy in the calm of universal peace is attested by all historians and by famous poets; even the chronicler of Christ's gentleness deigned to bear witness to it; and finally Paul called that most happy state "the fullness of time." Truly that time was "full," as were all temporal things, for no ministry to our happiness lacked its minister. What the state of the world has been since that seamless garment was first rent by the talon of cupidity we can read about would that we might not witness it.[35]

Any attack on the empire in its role as the *katechon* will from now on take shape as a real clash of civilizations, according to a dialectic which continues to this day. The *katechon*, moreover, does not tire of reappearing again and again in history: as occurs, for example, many centuries later when Luther identifies the Antichrist with the pope and the sumptuous apparatus of the pontifical court, a real aesthetic testimonial of the devil who lives there in the features of its supreme exponent. In its essence, even Luther's attack foreshadows a clash of civilizations, one that, moreover, sits completely inside the *civitas christiana* (or rather, the Christian confessions). Commenting on the famous passage from 2 Thessalonians, Luther writes emblematically: "The word 'Roman empire' was then transferred to the Germans, when there was no longer any trace of an empire; yet by this excuse that man exalted himself above all kings, above all bishops, above heaven and earth, and thus the kingdom was made firmer in his hand, after that, to validate this lie, the diploma of the donation of Constantine had also been invented, not only false but also stupid."[36]

He continues shortly after: "With this power of his *hidot* did he not perhaps create the new Roman empire, transferring it, according to him, from the Greeks to the Germans, which, if you like, is the most important and greatest offspring of all the works of the Antichrist? Who has not been convinced that these very great signs and these very great works came from God? While they were always very powerful and deceptive prodigies of Satan."[37]

If Calvin instead furnishes a positive interpretation of the *katechon* as an order that embodies the need to resist the apocalyptic through a power that avoids disintegration,[38] this step reveals that the history of the *katechon* stopped for a long time, finally reappearing with new features in the Russian thought and literature of the nineteenth century.

4

From Dostoevsky to Today

The Grand Inquisitor

It is in this context that the issue is newly addressed in its current form, in which problems concerning our present time emerge with increasing intensity. No matter how paradoxical it might seem, no symbol is more modern than that of the Antichrist. It must also be said that the Antichrist belongs to the genesis of the very idea of modernity that, at its core, would be inconceivable without it and the metaphors that belong to it. Moreover, without these metaphors, how would one be able to conceive of an age that wants to free itself from every dependency, a proudly and genetically illegitimate age, as it were, that does not want to recognize its relation with hypostasis or with the archetype?[1] We could say, particularly in light of the weight that Dostoevsky's *Grand Inquisitor* will take on in the context of the story of the *katechon* (through its late nineteenth- and early twentieth-century interpretations in the Russian context), that modernity is in some ways *the age of the complete substitution of the archetype with its double, the fictive or aesthetic age par excellence.* At least from this point of view, the Pauline metaphor remains extraordinarily effective in its capacity to decipher an epochal condition that it shares with the modern individual.

In the narrative of *The Grand Inquisitor*, which, as is well known, Dostoevsky entrusts to Ivan, the most complex and troubled of the three brothers Karamazov, Christ is rejected upon his return. His return has lost its meaning in the economy of the world, and perhaps even in that of all creation. In *The Grand Inquisitor*, happiness wishes to take primacy over conscience and truth. The fictitious double now seems to be present in every aspect of the story, achieving a devastating victory save for a truly absurd remainder, that of the suffering of the children, of those who have no culpability: a scandal so large that no theodicy can justify it. There is no longer a need for a messiah, and indeed he is frightening, disturbing a restless humanity that desires a quiet life, desirous of the most bourgeoise and philistine of peaces. The freedom that the Messiah announces, teaches, and intends to bring about by offering himself as a gift is an excessive gift, ultimately intolerable for a humanity that does not care for such restlessness. Humanity, in other terms, asks to be administered and directed. This is the very centre of the discourse which acts as a bridge and pivot point between the ancient and contemporary events of the *katechon*, and it is also the reason behind the extraordinary relevance of Dostoevsky's text today. By losing its historical and historical-religious specificity, the *katechon* becomes an unchanging anthropological variable and a category universally employable in the political debate. It is on these bases that Carl Schmitt was able to reinstate the timeliness of the term in the 1920s.

But are the *katechon* and legitimacy the same thing? Could they be considered in this way? It is rather clear that this shift (which *The Grand Inquisitor* represents in the most complete way) manages, in a decisive step, to transform the *katechon*. In the Pauline prophecy it represented the antagonist par excellence of the one legitimate lord and, at the same time, a transient but necessary passage, therefore in its own way legitimate, in the history of salvation. The inquisitor becomes the antagonist of the very Christ whom he should represent as an earthly vicar: Precisely by administrating his church, and by perpetuating its time indefinitely, he secretly pushes the Saviour away. The inquisitor is, therefore, more than the image of the fictive double, given that he imposes himself as the figure of absolute appearance. The *principium veritatis*, the Messiah, is deprived of its function: The Messiah no longer appears as the necessary hypostasis that cannot allow a double to exist alongside him, but rather as the legitimate principle which is no longer needed. The economic foundation (in a trinitarian key) of political power – as it was outlined in the preceding pages – is now definitively in crisis.

So let's take a look at *The Grand Inquisitor*. This sketch of a poem – this is how the author/narrator Ivan Karamazov defines it – set in Seville during the sixteenth century places the Roman Church, embodied by the terrible and austere figure of the grand inquisitor (just returned from a grandiose *autodafé*), in opposition to Christ who has returned to the world only to be immediately driven away by the one who ought to represent his message and guarantee his continuity. The spells of the Antichrist have overturned the Pauline dictums and warnings and defeated the Messiah himself, who in the end must distance himself, after having kissed the inquisitor, by abandoning an almost dumbfounded humanity which has declined to the point that it no longer has any sensibility and therefore no need for it: a humanity that has abdicated freedom and that is embarrassed by it as an excessive gift. It asks not to be saved, but to be guided, led by the hand, and, in a manner of speaking, administered. The men who have left the innocence of childhood behind and have tasted the fruit of the tree of good and evil thus tend to renounce this gift, and place it into the hands of those who know how best to use it: Freedom, upon closer inspection, is a true gift only for a few, solely for those who know how to raise themselves to the perfection of the will; for the others, it is an unbearable torment. The supreme task is to serve the happiness of humanity, the happiness of all incapable of handling the dizzying effects of freedom. Not surprisingly Alyosha, the youngest of the three brothers Karamazov, will tell Ivan that the inquisitor, whose story he tells, is, in reality, the devil.

This moment triggers an infinite series of interpretations that emphasize the diabolical ambiguity and duplicity of the

Antichrist. He never dismisses his similarity to Christ, thus triggering a dialectic of symbolic exchange between good and evil, but, above all, of an evil that needs fiction to represent itself and make itself plausible. All of this leads us, in an uninterrupted process, from Paul to the seduction of the market. This is noted by a famous interpreter of Dostoevsky, Nikolaj Berdjaev, who highlights how the Antichrist does not represent an ancient evil, but rather something that is absolutely new and current: "For the principle of Antichrist is not the old wickedness that springs to the eye in all its grossness: it is a new principle, refined, attractive, looking like goodness, and the superficial likeness between the evil antichristian principle and the good Christian principle is a source of great danger. The image of good begins to be 'divided,' Christ's image fades away and is merged into that of Antichrist."[2]

It will be in the dialogues dedicated to Vladimir Solovyov that the Antichrist, who will ultimately be revealed and beaten (according to the Pauline prophecy), appears under the guise of a father-master who serves humanity, now contented by the satisfaction of its needs and desires, through its pacification. In this age, when the divisions between the Christian churches will finally be overcome thanks to a great council, the fundamental impotence of Christ will emerge.

His challenge is unsustainable because his call to face the dizzying and restless abyss of freedom is unsustainable, replaced instead by a universal satisfaction of needs that seems to anticipate the socialist regimes. In the world of the Antichrist – which signals the victory of the empire over the papacy – a peaceful panorama of concord and philanthropy[3] is outlined, where the emperor is the president of the United States of Europe and a universal and complete satisfaction reigns: "So the nations of the world, after they have received from the Lord universal peace and universal abolition of hunger, were now given the possibility of never-ending enjoyment of the most diverse and extraordinary miracles."[4]

As Francesca Monateri highlights,[5] this is a case of obscuring the chaos under the principle of order inspired by *eudaimonia*.

This constitutes a sort of guiding thread within the Russian interpretations of the Antichrist, in a context that also emanates a Russian and orthodox pride equally hostile to the Catholic and the reformed world. This is what can be obtained from a great interpreter and friend of Dostoevsky like Vasilij Rozanov, whom we will deal with shortly. We are in the presence of a very sneaky and subtle transition: What opposes an invisible and therefore apparently inaccessible freedom is not a real order, which would require the idea of a realized justice, but, instead, a social organization able to dispense and relieve the majority of freedom.

Mystery has fled from in this world. But when the Enlightenment drives away the fairies (taking up E.T.A. Hoffmann's wonderful metaphor)[6] and bans mystery, freedom also suffers. Now everything must be made visible, completely evident to the point of a banality without any reserve, which rejects mystery rather than conceal it. *Now desire is configured as the desire for evidence that operates as a model.* It is a substantially pornographic model of power which reverberates almost literally through today's myth of transparency at any cost. Regardless of this passage (to which we will return to later), the impression here is one of an order imposed upon chaos. But it is necessary to focus on the idea of order. The regime of the invisible, known at least since Eusebius of Caesarea, is put on hold. That does not mean, however, that it is officially placed under question: rather, it is silenced. While recognizing the fundamental mechanism of the regime of the invisible as legitimate and the producer of legitimacy, it is compelled to spin aimlessly.

This is the trick, the point that heralds the actual formulation of the question and grounds it. The true confusion does not derive from chaos, from disorder of any variety – political, moral, social – but instead from the fact that it continues to certify the validity of a mechanism that, precisely while recognized and legitimate, is at the same time denied. In *The Grand Inquisitor* Christ really does return and his church should now be superfluous; but, in the end, the church rightly insists on its continued presence. It wants to organize an infinite transition, to represent Christ through the waiting for his return at the expense of the Christ who has finally returned. This shows that fomenting anomie is possible only by abandoning a legitimate order in exchange for a fiction. All of this is structured according to a very precise modality: It passes from a regime or from an economy of the invisible/visible to an economy that is totally visible, which seems to place any object of public or private desire, or both together, entirely at one's disposal. Social envy thus becomes the real motive that brings a community together.

The climate that is established here, in which Vasilij Rozanov plays a vital role, experiences the shared sensation of the imminent end – an end that has lost any messianic significance and gives in to a sense of universal degeneration and humbling prostration. The new humanity announced by the Messiah is replaced by a completely mediocre human example who asks only for a guarantee of some quiet and a bit of rest. Jesus is accused of not having thought about the happiness of humans despite the multitude of warnings that addressed this issue.[7] "It doesn't matter if you enslave us, just give us enough to eat,"[8] is the battle cry of those who confront the unhappiness that would tragically unfold from the freedom promised by Jesus, a freedom portrayed in exemplary fashion by the extreme solitude of the cross, which distanced the Messiah from humanity no less than it did from the Father.[9]

This tragedy already risks being overshadowed by the spectre of mass society. It outlines, in other terms, the spectre of the totally administered world which anticipates and saturates the desire of every individual – individuals who are not destabilized but comforted in their demands and in their real or presumed identity. Identity is defined here as a good of the highest order that has access to the market; the structure of demand is not one of need, but one of desire. From this point of view, we could say that there is no good that is not a symbolic good; in other terms, there exists no true use-value that is not also an exchange-value, to speak in Marxian terms. We are therefore dealing with a symbolic market.

Setting these themes aside – which we will cover in the final part of this book (and that develop slowly over a long period of time) – let us return to Rozanov, who claims that the inquisitor wants to be the modern caesar who dominates the world, almost predicting the global economy. But Rozanov also takes up, in an orthodox context, the traditional terms associated with the *katechon* since the commentaries of the Latin and Greek fathers,[10] as well as the polemical terms already taken up by Luther: The Antichrist is the pope himself. That claim notwithstanding, the Reformation is judged in absolutely negative terms (following a line that will also be – as we will see – taken up by Carl Schmitt) as an arbitrary uprising of subjectivity.

The rule of the inquisitor comes together as a paradigm of total submission to the point that crime is no longer conceived as such. For example, infanticide can be managed, in the name of cruel eudaimonism that benefits the community; even death and its significance are downplayed through the possibility of artificially inducing an end without pain.[11] But, more importantly, everyone under the rule of the inquisitor will be happy in the end. Humanity will encounter a process of programmatic regression that sweetly coaxes it to recapture the joy of childhood.[12] The actual rule of the inquisitor is rather mild. At the root of his command lies a deception, a devilish deception, persuasive and charming, that Paul announces in the Second Letter to the Thessalonians.[13] Ivan's discourse thus reveals itself to be demoniacal.

All of this reasserts, according to Rozanov, the centrality of the Orthodox Church, which verifies an intense communion with Christ without the burden of fictitious Catholic universalism and Protestant subjectivism.[14] On the other hand (and this is the crux of the question that also allows us to place it into perspective), in these pages Rozanov predicts the idea of the totally administered society, almost intuiting Horkheimer and Adorno's diagnosis from the *Dialectic of Enlightenment* about the link between totalitarianism and mass society. Rozanov says that science takes the place of education, signaling, even in the Russian context, the decline of the idea of *Bildung* that Nietzsche announced in his *Untimely Meditations* (and particularly in the second, *On the Advantages and Disadvantages of History for Life*) less than twenty years before the publication of Rozanov's essay on Dostoevsky. In other terms, we are dealing with a culture that no longer plays a formative role but functions instead like a technological apparatus, or a detailed schematic of useful notions for controlling nature and, more generally, the world surrounding it. The aestheticism of modern culture derives from a disintegration of *Bildung*, of culture itself insofar as it represents an ideal of a comprehensive education, extending to all spheres of behaviour but always in harmony with itself: a kind of real *imprinting* that was in some ways analogous to the *katechon*.

The Actuality of the Antichrist

And so we find ourselves before an entirely paradoxical transition, a peculiar atavism. Modernity here comes into contact with the most obscure of prophecies, as if it were dealing with the womb that generates it, or at least with the archetype that produces its fundamental outlines. At first glance it would seem unheard of to place the Antichrist into relation with modernity and its crisis. And yet these two things really are connected and hold together on the level of a metaphorical and (regardless of any dogmatic assumptions) truly prophetic power in the figure of the Antichrist. In this context, the critique and analysis of mass society – to express it here paradoxically and make the terms of the question more current – are almost paired together as a precognition contained in the metaphor of the Antichrist, *revealed here in all of its atheological, secular, and worldly power.* This allows us to see our present as a universe that embodies, develops, and carries to fulfillment a metaphorical constellation, almost as if it were the delayed germination of an ancient seed.

All of that – confirmed by some of the more recent Italian interpreters like Massimo Cacciari and Giorgio Agamben – matures in a context where the end, understood in an anti-utopian and anti-messianic key, feels ever closer. Rather symptomatic, in this context, is the letter that the Llerbach of Solovyov writes to his friend Gollerbach on 26 October 1918, toward the end of the First World War, almost as if to summarize the long wave of Dostoevskian teaching: "Everything is broken, broken, broken. There are no seeds left, everything is empty and stinks; the homeland is gone, it is empty, nothing is erased. Never believe in anything! But believe in life. And when an empty and nauseating place the size of a pea appears in the place of what is now dead, know that there is the germ, the resurrection."[15]

We could really say, with Agamben in *The Time that Remains*, that we finally realize that the coveted end of time is replaced with the time of the end, a sort of contradictory evocation of the end as the frightening but unavoidable event that pervades our time, whose scientific version could be Fukuyama's already mentioned "end of history."

An epochal transformation now occurs, which in the waiting for the end constructs an anti-utopian dimension, the projection of a completely negative future that replaces the final fulfillment. In this landscape the end does not reconnect with the beginning as it does in the messianic plan. To say it bluntly, there is no energy left to continue. But there is the disappearance of the end as the end and the announcement of an energetic collapse that prepares the transition mentioned above, one that leads to a sort of economy of desire: as if a time of momentary desire replaces the certainty of the return of the Risen, thus establishing a fast-paced economy which *shortens* the future, almost out of fear, expunging it from the places where the meaning of existence and history are constructed. All of this represents, obviously, a real collapse for a subject who, for centuries, constructed its own identity on the basis of the relation between the present, past, and future. In this framework, which indicates a radical systemic transformation, we come to recognize how Paul's words from the Second Letter to the Thessalonians continually predict our current situation. The messianic magic burns out and is confounded by the phantasmagoria of the present, where *the prize is no longer salvation, but certainty about oneself.*

In order to come to a provisional conclusion about this really fundamental stage in the story of the withholding power, it should be noted that it is precisely the "divine economy" that falls apart, which on the level of the Greek patristics (and in particular of the Cappadocian Fathers, according to Agamben's analysis in *The Kingdom and the Glory*)[16] institutes a sort of ontological circularity that summarizes the divine, trinitarian economy in the cosmicity of a power that searches for glory by faking, according to the etymological meaning of *fictio*, the messianic *eschaton*. Legitimate power is established by recapitulating the trinitarian story in its own structures, thus retracing the intra-divine messianic rhythm over the long time of the history the eternal return of the Son in the Father through the medium of the Holy Spirit. This produces a continuous cycle without interruptions or losses. From this point of view, human *perfectio* reflects the creation, as Hans Urs von Balthasar will recall much later in his monumental *Gloria*.[17] The prefiguring of the eschaton is moreover inserted within the messianic event that certifies and verifies worldly power and, at the same time, relativizes it. This type of power always and necessarily concerns, on closer inspection, what is second. In this sense the *katechon* performs a positive role by recognizing its secondary status in relation to the kingdom. Nevertheless, when the *katechon* dies – in the ideal itinerary that runs from Dostoevsky to Carl Schmitt – a sarcastic, mocking *hysteron proteron* comes to be: the second becomes the first, the representative becomes the represented and thus erases its presence and symbolic significance.

It is as if God were to disappear behind its own representations. The church takes the place of the Christ that it is supposed to represent. These same representations become idolatrous: The image is identified with what it represents and replaces it. This is the hysteron proteron: this exchange of the last with the first to produce an aestheticization of the world, ultimately negating the symbolic significance of the very figure it represents. Every vicariate is extinguished, and with it the very supremacy of Christ. If the representative comes to be identified with what it represents, the symbolic diaphragm fails. Thus we are dealing with an ideological figure, one of pure appearance that lacks a substance to feed it, and as such, remains illusory. Aestheticization is quite simply the result of this inversion between the representative and the represented, the culmination of the catastrophe wherein the symbolic sinks to substitute, to a vicarious figure, establishing itself as an apparently full presence that in reality is completely fictitious.

Precisely because the relation is directly felt, because the power of the symbolic dies, the king is naked from the start. The exchange between the representative and the represented produces a completely ideological power, a power that does not allow delegations to third parties. Here arises the shape and form of every charismatic leader, which includes the most recent ones belonging to the wave of populism. They leverage their charisma to the detriment of institutions, which fall apart when their appeal fades. They are leaders condemned to become obsolete rather quickly and to be replaced by other anodyne and equally precarious figures. Nevertheless, if this works to the detriment of the current power, if it places its fundamental structures into crisis, it then favours a market that constantly produces goods that cannot saturate subjective desire: goods that seem to grant the subject some compensation for its symbolic void but instead only expand it (as the market needs to produce other objects that meet the same need). We are dealing with a melancholic market, with an absolutely functional melancholia of the market. The terror of falling into anonymity produces goods that are increasingly characterized by the subject who wants to possess them (one thinks of Lapo Elkann's idea of personalizing one's own Ferrari); the subject cannot avoid being exhausted by this quickly, as in fact happens every time that we realize who we are and manage to satisfy the most basic narcissistic impulse – gazing at ourselves in a mirror.

In conclusion, let us return to Dostoevsky. By taking the place of the Saviour, of Christ himself, the inquisitor initiates a new figure: It erases the symbolic importance of the model and presents itself as the embodied reality of what/the one who dispenses salvation as survival and satisfaction, and thus also cancels, with the erasure of transcendence, the legitimacy of its own power. But the coup and the substitution are not obvious; nor could they be, since the catastrophe would otherwise take with them those who caused it or at least profited from it. The legitimate power is constantly betrayed and dispossessed of its own prerogatives, but never questioned regarding its transcendence. The glorious profile of legitimate power,[18] its epiphanic structure, is replaced by its new secondary, and yet also aesthetic, characterization. The epiphanic *auctoritas* of the legitimate sovereign is replaced by the prestige of the momentary leader: Prestige supplants *auctoritas*. The aestheticized representation entirely produces the aestheticization of power, which makes it completely unstable. If we examine our current moment, the charismatic leader who stands solely on a presumed prestige, whether real or totally fabricated, is always illegitimate and thus always exchangeable. Lacking any transcendent legitimization, the leader must find it through an unmediated mystical immersion in the most abstract and unstable of identities – that of the people. At the same time, the leader in this way also replaces the regulating power, the theological-political legitimization.[19] We have thus entered the *illegitimate age*, the epoch that lends its name to this book.

5

Still in the Christian Era

Seeing or Looking at Images?

Perhaps it is useless to highlight how closely this unredeemed humanity, which betrayed Christ guided by its pursuit of happiness, resembles Nietzsche's description – as Massimo Cacciari points out[1] – of "the last man" in *Thus Spoke Zarathustra*. Even here what emerges is the pursuit of happiness understood as the narcissistic saturation of a desire that savours its own fulfillment. As Zarathustra claims, the last man is the one who believes he has invented happiness. He is the smallest man, the one who survives the longest.[2] Ultimately, he is the one who has made desire, in its originarily inextinguishable quality, something that is finally commensurable and that can be immediately satisfied in the market. The last man (diametrically opposed to the overman) is the one for whom the earth has become too small, the one who has finally, after the death of God, conquered the mystery of the unknown.

This modern or late-modern anti-Ulysses substitutes the economy of desire for one based on the satisfaction of needs. While needs are partially extinguishable, the economic function of desire, insofar as it is reduced to a want, is always inextinguishable in its connection to the expansion and self-certification of the self: Since *individuum est ineffabile*, the desire cannot avoid being reborn after every one of its objections, after every certainty. In this way one's own self, identity itself, becomes a value introduced to the market. The satisfaction of desire has, above all, a narcissistic quality: the contentment of identity, the full and satisfied self-affirmation and self-understanding of the self. In this movement, where the anxiety of desire is lessened, the elephantiasis of subjectivity acts as a counterpoint, becomes the real supreme value, the foundation *in nuce* of what will become the neo-liberal economy. In contrast or parallel with the reduction of the earth's diameter, the last man can, in the end, be dilated and dilate his own ego thanks to an economic expansion of the self on the basis of social appearances, that is, on the basis of prestige.[3] What develops is no longer, at least principally, an economy of needs, but instead – as was suggested – an economy of desire that coincides with the social imaginary.

Here it seems that the parable of the Antichrist concludes or comes true as the eternal story of the exchange of the authentic self with the fictional one, as the granting of the true and usurped sovereignty. The death of God obviously hovers in the background, an extremely ambiguous and ambivalent event, which follows the Christian *kerygma*, the announcement of the risen God who was killed by the same humanity who ironically rejects him ("God is dead and we have killed him," as aphorism 125 tells us in *The Gay Science*). Here messianic time seems to reach its end. No one speaks any longer of the risen and his return. The double fiction, however, has taken his place. It is the modern Antichrist, the apostle of the end of history, overcome by the triumph of a subjectivity nourished by its own desire and suspicious of the future. The breath of messianic time ceases. The death of God announces the end rather than the beginning of a redeemed time.

The disappearance of the archetype produces an anthropological metamorphosis. The heroic subject and the conquest of the world characteristic of early modernity no longer takes precedence and is replaced by a desire that can be nourished and satisfied. In other terms, we are moving toward the aesthetic capitalism which I discussed at the beginning of this book in reference to Gernot Böhme. Desire and its satisfaction have become the principles of a social dynamic and the self-recognition of the subjects who are involved in it. This inexhaustible dynamic replaces the heroic solitude of the modern subject who lived in an estranged space where the distinction between universal needs and subjective desire were clearly delineated. In this new framework, need appears as impersonal while desire is personal and amplifies the subject. The modern structure of capitalism seems therefore to be oriented – in paradoxical conformity with the crisis of the *katechon* – toward an aestheticization of the self (and perhaps of the world) which also reverberates in an aesthetics of prestige: the exact opposite of the auratic aesthetics of the *katechon* in its sacredness.

Prestige exhibits, demands, and takes substance from light, never admitting anything that remains invisible; the *katechon*, conversely, depends on the invisible and makes the invisible its strength. From this point of view, the Pauline prophecy seems to have fully come true in our time – *an only apparently secular transition which in reality belongs to the profound history of the Christian era*, which even includes the atheism that has always been part of it. In short, the secular age – to invoke the title of Charles Taylor's great book[4] – lies entirely within the Christian era as its almost ironic counterpart. On the other hand, the entire story that we have been trying to trace up to this point seems to agree fully with Marcel Gauchet, according to whom Christianity is the religion of the end of religion.[5] If one were to appropriate this thesis and cross it with the more than thousand-year debate that we have traced so far, one could almost claim that secularization in the proper sense never existed, that the disenchantment of the world was never fully realized. The secular process, in other terms, has always held God within itself, as at least a metaphorical presupposition, without which it would never be able to function. Undoubtedly, we are dealing with an idea of God as archetype, but – as Carl Gustav Jung observed during his own time – it is precisely the archetype that makes itself felt with an intensity at least equal to that of its loss.[6]

Through this point of access we enter into the heart of the problem. If everything is visible, the archetype blinds itself – the light has gone out and it is no longer necessary. This is the true death of God: the disappearance of the invisible. Naming all of the devastating consequences this has for the modern conception/s of political power is certainly impossible. If the final presupposition has become completely and no longer solely partially invisible, then we have to go to other side: to imagine what it means to constitute a power no longer built using a top-down model, which begins with the presupposition of God and moves toward the human community, but using one that is bottom-up, which, starting with these empirical or empirical-transcendental assumptions, moves from the social body and its components to acquire its own legitimacy.

Returning to the history of the *katechon*, after these reflections it becomes clear, at least according to the outline proposed thus far, that the truly fundamental stage in the entire story is not the final but the penultimate one – an insight presented by an important historian, thinker, and conservator like Ernst Kantorowicz, the contemporary of Carl Schmitt, who not surprisingly fled to the United States to escape the evils of national socialism. In *The King's Two Bodies*, his most famous work, Kantorowicz proposes a theory of the legitimization of power that goes hand in hand with the idea of its unavoidably theological configuration. In the long itinerary of this book, the idea of a physical-spiritual configuration of the body of the king emerges. Such is the case, for example, with Edward VI, who possesses an earthly body that made him the holder of his lands, and a spiritual body which was the body of the real body politic. Kantorowicz writes: "The King's Two Bodies thus form one unit indivisible, each being fully contained in the other."[7]

Naturally, at the centre of all of this is a translation of the theological and canonical doctrine that is transferred from the ecclesiastical realm to the political-constitutional one,[8] supporting an antidocetist Christological model founded on the effective double nature, divine and mortal, of Jesus. From this point of view, a depicted theological hypostasis to which the image refers is necessary – to take up Marie-José Mondzain – in order to avoid its substantialization. In the opposite case, the image would be identified with what it portrays, losing its invisible boundary and thereby removing its iconic character.[9] If the image is substantialized, the freedom of the gaze falters and the image assumes an idolatrous aspect:[10] In other terms, it ends up overwhelming the gaze with its power. As Mondzain says further on: "A community gives itself an iconic vocabulary that allows it to identify the figures of its desire, and thus of its freedom."[11] She goes on to say that in the encounters gathered from images, a crossing of gazes is what constitutes the visible.

In the image, a relation between desire and freedom is thus instituted that grounds all of the transit through it. Moreover, this status of the image at the same time also guarantees the plurality of the gazes that are oriented toward the visible and guided by their desire. As one can ascertain from this passage, we therefore are not dealing with a leap to what was defined as the society of the image or aesthetic capitalism where the freedom of the gaze is connected to the impossibility of saturating desire, of seeing in an exhaustive way what one sees because behind the visible there constantly hides an invisible that produces it and, in some way, hides behind its facade. Relying on a wonderful paradox, Mondzain writes: "… the image exists, invisible and true. The fabricated and unredeemed visibilities harm the originary image; once redeemed, they open the gaze of free subjects …. The question of the image is not founded on objects, but on the nature of the gazes directed toward them. These gazes pertain to desire, and the passion of seeing must mourn its object. It leaves us to consider the nature of the objects we fabricate, and which of them are preserved in respect to this loss, or which, on the contrary, want to fill a void by killing desire, since they satisfy it."[12]

The Society of the Image after the *Civitas Christiana*?

Only in light of these reflections can we arrive at the final stage of the historical event of the *katechon*, which more closely involves, through Schmitt and Benjamin, modern power, especially considering the very wide debate on the *Ausnahmezustand*, on the "state of exception." Here we will limit ourselves to a few observations that will help set up the issue before it is treated more extensively in the final part of the book.

We have seen that the history of secularization is completely apparent, and this is not only because it helps to bring about a powerful rebirth of the religious and/or a widespread religiosity, but also, and above all, because it has not in fact departed from the theological economy that ruled the Christian centuries. The society of the image does not refute it, but instead perpetuates it by exasperating it and emphasizing its traits. The embodiment of many identities in the market indefinitely multiplies the event of desire, of recognition and self-recognition, which is the originary dialectic of the image. The mechanism seems to be blocked, or rather, continues to reiterate its own movement neurotically by organizing an important part of the economic system around the economy of desire. The neurotic state is paradoxically fully functional within the established economic regime. The allure, the attractiveness, and the effectiveness (however negative) of the withholding power do not fail: It acts powerfully through the universal melancholia obtained from its insistent and palpable absence.

We can therefore say that the fascination with the invisible continues to captivate the modern mind, which tries to pierce it from every side: from the point of view of the artistic gaze (one thinks of painters like Gerhard Richter), but also from the point of view of scientific research, which increasingly finds itself within the trajectory of the genetic gaze; from the point of view of a gaze that on many levels becomes ever more immodest and hunts for a mystery that sadly falls apart as it goes along.[13] The invisible has not decommissioned its attractiveness, but has simply spread it widely, and for this reason it seems more easily tamed. "Pierce the visible" has become the reverie of an age that wants to realize the impossible and always-fleeting dream of the naked king. The naked king, nevertheless, does not want the job; he is, in reality, a Masaniello who would like to dress himself in kingly garb and thus is not a true king but a rabble-rouser or a dictator. He will have to put on fictitious clothes to appear like the *true* sovereign, in this way unwittingly perpetuating the event of the *katechon* – or rather, the event of its disintegration.

What is proposed here is therefore the awareness that democracy (or at least pluralism) is impossible without a theological background that in fact has been more or less secularized. Only upon an invisible foundation is pluralism conceivable. The background is invisible, which makes possible a multiplicity of gazes that are not ensnared or captured by the object (which is what happens in an idolatrous system, therefore under the dictatorship of the subject who stands firm and assumes the power of a magic objectivity). Considerations of this nature certainly do not at all imply a slide back into theocratic power. On the contrary: It defends and protects the invisible layer of visible power, however one wants to conceive of it, so it does not fall into the obscenity of populisms that continually display the "symbolic" leader in flesh and bone (or possibly even in a bathing suit ...). This assumption is fundamental for grasping the nature of the present. Democracy, or at least pluralism, is tied to a sort of respect for the visible. This leads to the reassertion of the substantial continuity between the event of the *katechon* and our current situation, as Carl Schmitt astutely noted, by nevertheless accepting that from this happy intuition fateful consequences will follow, namely, clinging to an impossible dream in the hope that the powers of the *civitas christiana* might survive the collapse of the world they created without falling apart.

In this context one can also propose the theme of that apparent cataclysm – which is not a cataclysm at all – represented by the society of the spectacle[14] or by the society of the image. On the one hand it becomes clear that the unavoidable course of a society of the image is not unexpected but, at least in its paradigms of meaning, completely intrinsic to a historical event that extends over a long time, the collapse of which this society records melancholically. This restores a perspective on the present that, in some themes and moments of contemporary thought, seems to have fallen into a bottomless impoverishment of its own symbolic resources; where the event does not seem to correspond to a sinking, but rather to the fulfillment of a truly prophetic mechanism from the point of view of the precision of its mechanism's functioning. Two aesthetic models are placed into continual contrast and constantly reappear: that of the *katechon*'s plastic power, to which Schmitt still seems to give credit,[15] and that of the aesthetic transformation of capitalism, on which we will dwell more exhaustively in the final part of the book.

Naturally, in this context, it is the evaluation of aestheticism that holds its ground, where it does not at all constitute a critical zone where reality is clouded over, but its exact opposite: a new economic and ontological *status* whose functionality is powerful and very obvious. Aestheticism, briefly, does not at all signify derealization – which, for example, is suggested by the title of Heidegger's essay, "The Age of the World Picture"[16] – but rather the recognition (by now largely acquired) of the image's performative nature and, on the other side, its role as the backbone of self-recognition. In other terms, this is the outcome of an ego that seeks to be universalized in the absence of a founding power of the *katechon*. This propensity to become icons stabilizes the catechonic residue in its ordering and validates its performative, and even creative, character in the face of political reality. The image thus functions performatively, both prefiguring and implementing a desire that definitively modifies its ontological status.

It is an image that – according to Benjamin's hypothesis in *The Origin of German Tragic Drama* – becomes allegorical, pursuing future time as a reason for self-recognition and fulfillment:

an image in its own way still messianic. To the extent that it embodies a desire and an identity, it functions as the motor of the entire process, rendering it perpetually unstable, incapable of reaching a symbolic turning point like the *katechon*. When Benjamin sent *The Origin of German Tragic Drama* to Schmitt in 1930, not only did he recognize the debt he owed to him, but also that he had greatly and amicably surpassed him by pointing out to Schmitt the limits of his perspective.[17] Benjamin wrote that in his book he was developing on the aesthetic level what Schmitt had been developing on the political level. From this we can infer an implied meaning that is perhaps more meaningful than what was only explicitly stated: Benjamin wanted to express something more profound than a simple tribute. Behind the tribute and the recognition of a profound affinity one easily finds an objection, almost an indication of an argument, precisely an aesthetic one, developing from a point of view that effectively belongs to it and, in the end, subsumes the others. This will be the turning point for the entire issue, which will allow us to head into the latter part of this book with an adequate background.

Before reaching this point, it should be emphasized that rarely does a brief biblical passage like the second paragraph of the Second Letter to the Thessalonians carry so much weight, even in secular history, in its relation of proximity and distance to the sacred. The aesthetic, or if one prefers, creative potential of the *katechon* that we have tried to follow in the preceding pages, despite any residual hope from Schmitt, has exhausted its own event, leaving us standing before a profound void. There is no relation between the *katechon* and the state of exception, as Schmitt tried to demonstrate, because the *katechon* is not a concrete check on nihilism; nor does nihilism in itself represent something absolutely negative – as Benjamin emphasizes in his essay *Toward the Critique of Violence*, where he once again confronts Schmitt. *Reine Gewalt*, the "pure violence" which Benjamin defends,[18] makes it so that – as we will see later – it defines an entirely positive dimension of nihilism, which refers to a destruction that institutes or restores an alternative time – the messianic one. Nihilism would thus seem to be the verification (and not, as in Dostoevsky and Nietzsche, the negation) of the messianic request inherent in Paul's text and in the commentaries that follow. Finally (and based on Benjamin's directions), a poetics of ruin takes shape here, which is added to the prior aesthetic specifications of political theology.

Autonomy (of the Politician) Denied

This path radically questions the idea or the ideal of the autonomy of the politician, who instead becomes prisoner to a model of legitimization derived from theology that remains valid no matter how gangrenous it has become. The autonomy of the politician, pursued like a dream or a nightmare in the 1970s,[19] gives way to a politics completely subjugated to the aesthetic logic of goods, for which the leader is also an actor and the actor is also a leader. In this framework, a fundamental question still needs to be asked. Couldn't there be an opportunity for a different creative organization of politics that no longer moves in the top-down manner of the *katechon*, whose form is by now disintegrated, but in a bottom-up movement of a politics that is founded on a new creativity, a sort of *reinvention of democracy*? This would entail – as Santiago Zabala has pointed out – taking a cue from the situation created by populisms to replace the "outdated" charisma of the populist leader with different forms of authentication for the self and for the leader.[20]

Moreover, the choice proposed here is not one between the *katechon* and ruin, which would seem to emerge in the distant comparison between Benjamin, Taubes, and Schmitt. In some way even Schmitt recognizes an aesthetic element in the principle of the dissolution of the *katechon*, where the Protestant *Affekt*, the individualistic soul of the Protestant faith (and Lutheranism in particular), is contrasted with the public vocation of Roman Catholicism.[21] Here is the Hegelian objection to individual subjectivity lacking substance, to a nominalist inclination of modernity, which in an only apparently paradoxical way brings the critique of Protestantism closer to that of Romanticism. In the end, both aspects have much to do, at least implicitly, with the question of the *katechon*. The sin of Protestantism is in other terms the interiorization of the faith that desymbolizes it.[22]

One can trace a common thread stretching from *Political Romanticism* to *Roman Catholicism and Political Form* that concerns the critique of modernity, or, more precisely, its inclination toward the individual that in ancient terminology was defined as nominalism. This is the real anarchic threat that manages to keep the impending chaos within itself; it comes from afar. The model that Schmitt instead has in mind – as *The Nomos of the Earth* testifies – is that of the *respublica christiana*, which is not proposed in opposition to the Roman Empire, but in substantial continuity with it.

Before appearing in *The Nomos of the Earth*, this idea was outlined in four essays from 1922 that mark the origin of Schmitt's conception of the *katechon*. Here a thoroughly modern relation derived from theological categories emerges that conflicts with that of Hans Blumenberg, who would establish an intense dialogue with Schmitt on the basis of his substantially neo-Enlightenment vision of modernity as marked by a clear break with the past.[23] Therefore, we are dealing with a retro-dating of modernity that affects its Enlightenment foundations. Modernity in this framework does not represent a Kantian "release from [man's] self-incurred tutelage,"[24] but, instead, the decline of the order founded on the *katechon*. This produces conceptions of representation and political pluralism diametrically opposed to each other. And it is precisely this aspect which matters the most today. Schmitt writes about these issues in some of the most cited passages from his work: "All significant concepts of the modern theory of the state are secularized theological concepts not only because of their historical development – in which they were transferred from theology to the theory doctrine of the state ... but also because of the systematic structure, the recognition of which is necessary for a sociological consideration of these concepts."[25]

In the concrete spatial localization in relation to Rome, and already in general norms and ideas, one then finds the continuity that ties the international medieval right to the Roman Empire. An essential feature of the Christian empire was that it was not an eternal kingdom, but instead always kept in mind its own end and the end of the present epoch, and despite that was able to exercise its power historically. The decisive and historically important concept was that of the "withholding power" (*Aufhalter*) of the *katechon*: "'Empire' in this sense meant the historical power to *restrain* the appearance of the Antichrist and the end of the present eon; it was a power that withholds (*qui tenet*), as the Apostle Paul said in his Second Letter to the Thessalonians."[26] Schmitt also recalls that "the emperor claims *auctoritas* and the pope claims *potestas*."[27] The error would consist in what happens beginning from the thirteenth century, when "the Aristotelian doctrine of the *societas perfecta* [perfect society] was employed to divide the church and the world into two types of societies."[28]

This foreshadows a horizon in which utopia and nihilism cross each other. The *societas perfecta* enters into conflict with the idea of the transient empire that declines with the realization of the messianic plan. It is clear that in this context the one true enemy of the order dispensed by the *katechon* is – referring again to Paul's statement – the messianic anxiety that wears out and destroys the *civitas christiana*, upsetting its equilibrium and boring into it with the unspeakable worm of eschatology, which now takes on the form of nihilism. Not surprisingly, when Schmitt dwells on the *nomos* of the earth and its characteristics, he rejects any sanctioning of those features with the abstract concept of the law. Moreover, every disorder within the empire does not promote a dissolution of its structure, also because the *katechon* was not going to be embodied in a figure precisely defined from the beginning by rank or by family lineage. No disorder within the empire could produce the modern break known as nihilism. And Schmitt reveals how only a "completely different spatial order" could produce the meltdown that was defined as nihilism and had nothing to do with the moments of anarchy in the Middle Ages. The emergence of nihilism had to be a kind of messianic crypto-rebirth that produces some sort of uprooting and delocalization, an equivalence between nihilism and utopia. Schmitt writes: "In the connection between *utopia* and *nihilism*, it becomes apparent that only a constitutive and fundamental separation of order and orientation can be called 'nihilism' in a historically specific sense."[29] The nomos derives from a felicitous joining of ordering and localization.[30] Schmitt defines it using a formulation that closely resembles Heidegger: "Nomos comes from *nemein* – a [Greek] word that means both 'to divide' and 'to pasture.' Thus, nomos is the immediate form in which the political and social order of a people becomes spatially visible – the initial measure and division of pastureland, i.e., the land-appropriation as well as the concrete order contained in it and following from it. ... Nomos is the measure by which the land in a particular order is divided and situated; it is also the form of political, social, and religious order determined by this process."[31]

What emerges is a wholly substantial concept of nomos that is tied to localization as possession, which excludes any juridical formalism. On this basis we are aware that the same transformation of nomos into law produces an uprooting that can only be defined as nihilism.

Nihilism thus coincides with a reading of the messianic call that identifies the modern as an uprooting, as the illegitimate age, as the place of anomie; an age in which there is a sort of equivalence between utopia and atopia. Uprooting becomes the equivalent of societal uneasiness, where the suspicion of a renewal of the messianic utopia within the context of the Soviet revolution is brought to our attention, a renewal which in turn was quickly thwarted. Schmitt's conception, even though anti-democratic, cannot be defined as anti-pluralistic, where it is precisely the primacy of a unique principle that allows for the fulfillment of the variegated terrain of cultural and local differentiations. Schmitt's polemic turns against the tyrant and tyranny, against what he defines as Bonapartism, almost as if we were dealing with a degraded form of the *katechon* that almost takes on the guise of the adventurer and the leader of the people. In this context, Bonaparte dons the clothes of the imposter; Ingres's portrait of *Napoleon I on His Imperial Throne* is there to pay witness to him. Perhaps no figurative text can provide an interpretation of the disintegration and preposterousness of the *katechon* in today's world better than Ingres's painting, in which the sumptuous symbols of power seem overdone and almost theatrical.

The decadence of the *katechon* was underway, according to Schmitt, since the thirteenth century, where its clearly transient function fails. The emperor performs a function radically distinct from the king and the monarch, whose function is transitory – just as their reign is necessarily transitory and does not take the place of the Messiah, who wields the real power. The very legitimacy of the modern age is at stake here. The dispute between Blumenberg and Schmitt arises precisely on this level: it regards the definition of the modern and the question of the break that, according to Blumenberg, generates modernity due to the force of secularization. For Schmitt, modernity is not generated by a break:[32] The mechanisms of legitimization that define the Christian age still apply today. Modernity does not constitute a leap forward but is founded upon the memory of the ancient. We are always – following Schmitt – in the Christian *aion*; we are always in agony and every important event is nothing more than a matter of *katechon*.[33] According to Schmitt the nomos is analogous to the *temenos* – it localizes and delimits a *topos* by constructing an ethos. It is difficult not to notice in these theses an assonance with Heidegger's notion of *Geworfenheit*, the "thrownness" presented in *Being and Time*, which challenges the need to allocate another place beyond the desert of nihilism (a need described, for example, in the essay "The Origin of the Work of Art," where the work of art itself is understood as a modality of foundation by following up on the need for a new rooting).

Schmitt points out how the positivization of the law following 1848 produces a complete misrepresentation of the concept of nomos. The law is conceived as a procedure connected to a punishment where, on closer inspection, the nomos is essentially impossible to transgress as it is a rooting principle without which no legal framework exists (and without which there could exist no legal procedure). Even in this case the affinity that nomos shares with the concept of "being" in Heidegger is rather obvious. All of this develops in the context of a profoundly negative conception of modernity, as attest, among other things, both his small book *Roman Catholicism and Political Form* and his work *Political Romanticism*, which precedes it by a few years. In both cases, the negative principle of modernity is individuality, which places a nominalistic emphasis on chance, and, thus, on what is essentially uncontrollable and not subservient to the big *frame* of the nomos.

Individuum est ineffabile one more time means, after Hegel, that individuality does not have a foundation and cannot avoid sinking into its own solitude along with the epoch that created it. Nihilism is not, from this point of view, an originary phenomenon, but derivative, epigenetic: It is the child of the diffractive spirit of modernity, the age that accelerates time, that emphasizes its nature as the medium of signification through the idea of progress; that breaks the limits of the temenos, questioning every limit. In the disintegration derived from an excessive intensity and from the immense centrifugal force that drives the acceleration of time, a path forms.[34] Ruling over the particular thus becomes the problem of the age comprehensively more energetic than all others. The questions develop through a long circuitous passage, which first appeared timidly in post-Hegelian aesthetics, for example in the work of Friedrich Theodor Vischer which posed the problem of causality in relation to form, then emerged in a more noticeable and irrefutable way in Ernst Jünger's important essay dedicated to "Total Mobilization," and finally took on its definitive arrangement thanks to Schmitt's concept of *Ausnahmenzustand*, of the "state of exception."

The modern age is the one that cannot but create *idola* like Napoleon, heroes of a time that does not create *nomoi*, but *thesis*.

If there is something that, in this context, must be specified, it is precisely the concept of idol, which becomes important for identifying all of the upcoming passages in this book and leading all the way to the meaning of the idea of aesthetic capitalism. The idol is basically the result of the decline of the catechonic structure, the result of a *debacle* of the symbolic that no longer supports its own transcendent structuring but draws closer to the zero level, becoming immanent to the point of incarnating itself in the very body of the sovereign; the body thus turns into an eternal one, a living contradiction, precisely a fake god, an idol. The idol coincides in every way with the illegitimate sovereign, who has lost the transcendent foundation guaranteed to it by the *katechon*. Contrary to the legitimate sovereign, the idol can change its features at will, because it does not depend on an invisible process. It is the lookalike, the double of the legitimate sovereign, but also a shape-shifter; it can counterfeit the face of the true sovereign, and having no need for the true one, refers to ever-changing foundations (the masses, the nation, the people) apparently endowed with irrefutable evidence.

The issue is not a matter of simple reproducibility, but the possibility of producing a typology of what cannot be reproduced. The icons of Francesco Giuseppe mentioned by Musil did not by themselves constitute a diminished copy of the original since they constituted adequate typologies of it, copies that conform to the original, as faded or even counterfeited like Duchamp's moustache in *La Joconde*. Analogously, as we are told in E.T.A. Hoffmann's story *Der Feind* (*The Enemy*), what holds for the sovereign also holds for Albrecht Dürer: Anyone in Nuremberg who took home a hand-made copy of a painting by Dürer did not betray the original but shared in its aura.[35] On the contrary, we have now entered the age of the "technical" reproducibility of the sovereign, in which lookalikes (very noticeably counterfeit) of the authentic sovereign, or rather of authentic sovereignty, are reduced to psychological personalities, famous characters similar to those of the world of showbusiness, who attract for themselves and their private lives a morbid curiosity that quickly disappears once the curiosity is satisfied. This happens because the symbolic substance that supports sovereignty is irreparably lost: The sovereign is no longer a distinct type.

Undressing the king – which happens continually – now becomes a way of stripping him of his fake sovereignty. Here we can again consider the analogy between Mao and Marilyn highlighted by Warhol. The invisible body of the sovereign is transformed into an infinite, dazzling, reproducible icon, no doubt condemned to a rapid obsolescence. It is obvious that all of this leads to a confusion of roles: The sovereign is no longer such, but simply becomes a leader; and the leader, in turn, becomes a performer or a socialite. *High and low* are confused, thus opening the door for aesthetic capitalism which, lacking an identity endowed with a transcendent validation, produces individuals who simply self-validate by becoming their own spectacle, turning their own features into a symbol, recognizing their own value proposition precisely in the self-donation of a public and universal self. Art, precisely in the transition from the *readymade* to Warhol, discovers this passage, rejects it, and also corroborates it, by verifying, on the one side, the fall of the transcendentals and, on the other, the continuing and consequent interchangeability between high and low.

A new spiritual climate is created which overcomes all of Schmitt's expectations. The movement underway is not structured like a reissue of messianism, but, if anything, is like a repeated decline of the transcendence that claims its rights at ever lower levels. The choice is not between form (the *katechon*) and messianic ruin (according to a recurrent modality of interpreting the oppositional relation between the two), but instead a choice between the integral structuring of a world within a unique form or the re-declination of this form according to infinite variants, which modify and transform its shifting forms based on differing supports, but without ever fully distrusting its ability to remove the void and provide a definitive meaning. In the course of these migrations, the form tends to descend ever lower, passing from a transcendental structuring to the games played by Warhol, all the way to *embodiment*, to the desperate and yet hopeful clinging to tattoos on the skin of a significant portion of the younger population.

The Nomos and the Messiah

As is known, Schmitt addresses the issue of the nomos and of the withholding power not only in *The Nomos of the Earth*, but also in texts like *Land and Sea* (1942). His own vision was undoubtedly modified and transformed in the arc of this period; above all the model of beauty as the fundamental archetype of the *katechon*, according to a consonant relation of micro and macrocosm, resonates forcefully beginning with his book on *Roman Catholicism and Political Form*. But this is not the only solution present in Schmitt's thinking. After the Second World War Schmitt notes the possibility that the nomos is reborn from its ashes, following unforeseen paths, precisely in the present situation in which the imperium is interrupted thanks to the division between East and West.

What will the new nomos identified by Schmitt be? Might it perhaps be – to be mischievous – the new universality described by the thousands of late-modern identities, by the billions of ways, mediated and not, of saying "I"? Even in light of this extravagant, but probably in its own way relevant, consideration, within Christianity the *katechon* in this way comprises the great temptation to deny its own messianic vocation, its essential destination – to structure itself as the worldly *civitas*. This is the fundamental presupposition that arises from its history and, above all, from the analysis given in Schmitt's work and in the distant confrontation between him and the Jewish intellectual Rabbi Jacob Taubes. In the eyes of Taubes, not only did Schmitt defend the *katechon*, but he is himself the *katechon*. According to Taubes's *Occidental Eschatology*, the *katechon* over time comes to take possession of the

Christian story (as testified by, among other things, the progressive recognition of the mendicant, Franciscan, and Dominican orders). The *katechon* is diametrically opposed to the end of time, which Taubes also diagnoses in a series of lectures, given in Heidelberg, on *The Political Theology of Paul*, that constitute the final chapter of his work and of his life. In the intense confrontation with Carl Schmitt, born under the sign of conflict, the central issue is the question of whether the *katechon* should be valued positively or negatively. To oppose the *katechon*, Taubes and Benjamin propose a positive practice of nihilism. Taubes wrote: "This is what he [Schmitt] later calls the *katechon*: the restainer [*der Aufhalter*] that holds down the chaos that pushes up from below. That isn't my worldview, that isn't my experience. I can imagine, as an apocalyptic: let it go down. I have no spiritual investment in the world as it is. But I understand that someone else is invested in this world and sees in the apocalypse, whatever its form, the adversary and does everything to keep it subjugated and suppressed, because from there forces can be unleashed that we are in no position to control."[36]

In a parallel manner, already a decade before, Benjamin recognized in the communist revolutionary movement a tension and a mystical identity that was not confused with the religious one: "It is really imperative that we understand, in precisely its polemical bearing, the apotheosis of organization and of rationalism which the Communist party has to promote unceasingly in the face of feudal and hierarchical powers, and that we be clear about the fact that the movement itself comprehends mystical elements as well, although of an entirely different sort. It is even more important, naturally, not to confuse these mystical elements, which pertain to corporality, with religious elements."[37]

It is, for Benjamin and Taubes, a common framework in which the mystical is contrasted with religion, precisely because religion constitutes the anti-messianic construction par excellence, designed to manage the time of waiting, or the indefinite and contradictory prolonging of the time of the end. In the palingenetic view of Taubes, one geared toward the renewal of earthly hope, mysticism and revolutionary rationality thus come to be superimposed over and confused with each other. It is the panorama of the ruin of history running backwards from Klee's angel to project time into its own beyond, that of the final palingenesis, represented or substituted by the Soviet revolution (which emanates above all from some of the highest moments of the artistic avant garde).[38] The Benjaminian ruins that accumulate during the passing of the angel are allegories of the future looming behind the messianic promise: the reintegration of time and of the future times in the sign of the messianic promise that renews the palingenetic demand. The ruins of history are therefore not rubble, but instead presuppositions of the final reintegration; while the messianic culmination is protected in its mystery by the impossibility of the angel looking in the direction where the wind is taking it.[39] Here then is the *aesthetics or poetics of ruins and of the fragment* which we have already mentioned, as a premise to the renewal of the times.

And it is precisely on this basis that the resolute anti-messianism of Carl Schmitt, his significant bias for the *katechon* against the final fulfillment, becomes insightful. Paradoxically there arises a sort of substantial equivalence, in the Schmittian outlook, between messianism and nihilism. The surprising aspect is found in the fact that on the other side, from Benjamin to Taubes, the messianic hope seems to be renewed thanks precisely to the adoption of nihilism as a positive moment, which profits from the panorama of ruins over which the present directs its gaze. In this context the messianic hope unexpectedly renews its ancient vitality. The diagnosis concerning the critical moment embodied today is the same in the eyes of the two great interlocutors, Taubes and Schmitt, who nevertheless diverge radically when it comes to the prognosis, to their prospects on the future.[40] On the other hand, Benjamin emphasizes the total estrangement of messianism and religion. Benjamin also defines nihilism as "the method of world politics." This interpretation contradicts the interpretative event of nihilism,[41] traditionally seen as a moment of negative disintegration and not of regeneration. Benjamin writes in the *Theological-Political Fragment*, in tones that recall the palingenetic anxiety of early German Romanticism: "To strive after such a passing, even for those stages of man that are nature, is the task of world politics, whose method must be called nihilism."[42]

The political-messianic practice of nihilism thus uncovers the profound antithesis between the protagonists in this comparison, whose terms and aims were entirely clear to both. Decisive for Benjamin is the question of allegory elaborated in *The Origin of German Tragic Drama*, the idea of a process of historical events that does not have its meaning in itself, but rather in an elsewhere or beyond that constitutes its ultimate truth. It is worth considering (regardless of the instinctive sympathy that almost everyone probably has for the positions of Benjamin and Taubes) whether the alternative is definitive over the long term. There is, ultimately, a question whether there is a *tertium datur* that avoids nailing down the question in its original terms. This unforeseen prong of the issue could be represented by the hypothesis which proposes that both Schmitt's perspective along with the regenerative hope cultivated by Benjamin in light of the Russian revolution would run up against a necessary impasse. Both of them have turned in the direction of a catastrophic outcome, even though things would seem to have gone in an unforeseen direction, which is what I have tried to describe through the theme of aestheticization.[43]

Time teaches us that, in reality, we do not find ourselves standing before an unresolved choice between the *katechon* and messianic nihilism, to which Taubes returns with great force in his lecture "Carl Schmitt: Apocalyptic Prophet of the Counter-revolution."[44] Here it becomes clear that the choice between the two, almost like that between Benjamin and Schmitt, rests entirely in whether one takes a position that favours or resists the apocalyptic. Moreover – Taubes claims: "Christianity was for Schmitt 'Judaism for the people,' against whose power he was ever ready to rise up. But he saw more deeply how vain such a 'protest' against God and history would be."[45] If for Schmitt the Jewish people represent the true exponents of messianism, whose story involves, dangerously in his eyes, the contemporary culture, a paradox emerges: the incompatibility of religion and mysticism which was at first unforeseeable. The messianic vocation cannot be religious and also religion, as the institutional organization of faith, on its part, is not mystical. In this way – in the eyes of Taubes as critic of Schmitt – the stability of the *katechon* is superimposed over that of the religious. Religion is, in other terms, directed to slow down the ultimate outcome of the promise that it cultivated: the coming of the Messiah. The *katechon* presents itself as powerful in this context, offering the *chance* for an organization of religious power, fundamentally atheist, that rejects the messianic adventure to confirm the completely worldly stability of its structures and its symbols.

That notwithstanding, the messianic identity survives alongside the religious one, and neither of the two really manages to break away from the other. This gives rise to that *contradiction in adiecto* that defines our time. In its time, the idea of a *katechon* is reintroduced in the form of an *exemplum*, of a different symbolic image that anticipates and delays the end. We are dealing with an indefinitely prolonged attempt to reproduce, under new guises and forms, the legitimacy of the bond represented by the withholding power; an attempt that assumes an ever-accelerating rhythm, turned against a time that it warns is contradictory and ungrounded, that continually and iteratively wants to find confirmation in itself, thus producing a vast multiplication of previously obsolete figures that would nevertheless have to legitimate it. On this path the *katechon* will surely either explode or implode, depending on one's point of view. Even in this case, the aesthetic implications of the question made themselves known from the beginning. In a manner similar to what occurs in art, we are dealing with the form as the element capable of closing and, broadly, of concluding, of furnishing a meaning that is stable and not subject to excessive oscillations. The powerful translation of the Vulgate that renders the *katechon* with the *forma qui tenet* expresses these similarities and seems to present itself as a dynamically positive counterweight to a negative *dynamis*, a systematic instability, which – to use Ernst Jünger – marks the epoch of "total mobilization": an age so powerful, from an economic and political standpoint, it is crossed by centrifugal tensions that certify both its strength and its fragility.

On these bases, the need arises for a dynamic form already expressed by the German Romantics, a form in movement that is capable of grasping the *disiecta membra* of a universe in a state of constant becoming.[46] The proposals by Benjamin and Taubes instead lead us to an alternative option, but one no less noble and established in the aesthetic and philosophical tradition: the aesthetics of ruins. In this sense we can speak of a kaleidoscopic society that continually rearranges its own components. It is yet another element in the aesthetic composition of the *katechon*. The ruins represent a real hieroglyph: not, however, as the traces of a chthonic past that wants to rise again, as one sees in eighteenth-century ruins (think of Piranesi), but instead, like the alphabet, in the midst of composition, for a language belonging to a future yet to be invented. The messianic identity connected to the idea of the *katechon*, which had been hiding throughout most of its history, reappears in the end as a sort of removal and revelation in the full maturity of the historical-spiritual moment.

The practice of nihilism evoked by Benjamin understands the *katechon* as the end of history and announces another event to which we belong more intimately. Benjamin wants to reiterate that the beat of messianic time still continues to pulse today, and that it also represents the hermeneutic instrument that allows us to interpret the present. What is at stake in Benjamin and Taubes is the direction of messianic time, its ultimate meaning, an orientation that in the end times sees the *chance* for the *Erlösung*, for a redemption that is grounded upon a decisive act. It interrupts the monotonous procession of moments and introduces a new time. It is the idea of a time grounded on the *Jetztzeit*, on the moment that profits from the temporal ruins and takes an inaugural step. All of this comes together naturally and emerges at the same time thanks to the image of the angel of history from the fourth of Benjamin's *Theses on the Philosophy of History*, which, as I was saying above, traverses a panorama of ruins pushed by a wind that drives it forward even though it does not know where it is going, given that it moves backwards, from behind.

We are dealing, in no uncertain terms, with the proposal of a hermeneutics of the future. The ruins are the epigones of a catastrophe whose final meaning will be defined in a redeemed future, which generally takes shape as a real apocatastasis, as a total renewal of the times and a reintegration of the world in its Edenic state. The message is paradoxical in its crystalline purity. What looms behind it is the paradoxical idea of a messianic nihilism; the idea that resolutely excludes from its own horizon the most typical form of nihilism, that of *The Grand Inquisitor*, and the rather similar Nietzschean one, of "the smallest man," obscured by the multiplicity of small desirous impulses coursing through the late-modern subject.

Both choices – the catechonic and the messianic – as was stated above, nevertheless give way to an intermediate solution, one that is very ambiguous and perhaps also very rich. We are dealing with a powerful dissolution of the *katechon* that persists in a still more powerful form, that of contemporary aestheticism, the new sphere of the intelligence of power and modes of production. It is the Benjaminian aestheticization of politics that replaces or embodies today's Antichrist, as if to mark the economy of desire as the economy of social envy and of *diaballein*, the premise of contemporary populisms. Where identity becomes the supreme value, it is also presented as the locus of desire and of conflict. It must be emphasized that the two levels are intimately interconnected. From this point of view, the reflection on the *katechon* leads us not only beyond Schmitt and Benjamin-Taubes, but also beyond the formulations given in the Italian debate, committed to further elaborating the choice between messianism and the withholding power.

We could say that today the *katechon* often appears under both its messianic and catechonic forms. In other terms, we are dealing with figures that establish their legitimacy in a catechonic key, as

- their power reverberates in the sphere of an invisible-visible that constitutes or ought to constitute their aura: It is the ever more frequent case of a "direct" delivery of power to personalities who are well-known (and rightfully so) for their prestige and their competence.
- they are attributed with (perhaps despite every intention of their own) a messianic identity that makes them saviours.

This connection inevitably produces the death of the same catechonic identity, by thus moving these personalities (again, despite their intentions) closer to populistic leaders and producing, sooner or later, their unavoidable decline. The palingenetic call constantly and explicitly re-echoes in populist leaders by grounding the non-institutional legitimacy of their power. The catechonic appeal to the invisible, under the species of a poorly popular will, co-exists with the palingenetic idea of a leader ready to take the place of the Messiah. The institutional legitimization of his power follows the recognition of this palingenetic identity. Every one of these leaders in their turn reproduces, in an iterative fashion, that desire for symbolic identity that ends up imploding or also exploding in the universe of the society of the image.

In the universe where the hunger for images is ever more intense, there appears, on closer inspection, an elusive desire for self-affirmation and legitimization at the same time. Foundational images are projected – legitimate identities that become increasingly obsolete, confused, and numerous, prisoners of a mechanism that make the image itself its principle good. Identity is now aware of its reflection in its images, which thus take on an increasingly high value and an ever more intense meaning.

They are increasingly connected not only to the elevated forms of self-representation of the self which were mentioned earlier, but also, and perhaps still more, to motives connected to the biological survival of individuals.

Food constitutes an exemplary case in this framework. Slow Food demonstrates this *ad abundantiam*, and nevertheless with many excellent reasons: Food is its history; it feeds us through its biological as well as its symbolic body, which is often narrated and presented to us by the restaurateur. The "legitimizing" images lose any transcendent formulation and tend to invest in their own body with increasing intensity. Moreover, this is normal: As Hans Belting teaches in *An Anthropology of Images*, the transmission of images is organized structurally in the triad image-medium-body.[47] In the case of food, as is also the case (in different terms) with tattooing, the image has lost its distance from its medium, reset it to zero, so much so that it is even embedded in or introjected into it. The more this distance is reduced, the more power the image acquires – as testified by the artist who imagines and portrays ferocious and monstrous mobile phones that engulf those who become immersed in them.

Identity, captured in the image, is a true good driven by the market, whether it be an ID, a green card, luxury, or fashion. In all of these cases the image appears as a good connected to our most elementary need: knowing who we are. Identity is sold and driven on the market as the most precious value. They are identities in images, which impose themselves and get recognized. They are persistently required to regulate the global Babel and to supply – it is said again and again – identity and orientation. Nevertheless, they remain hostages to the same mechanism that produces them and that feeds the (their) market: They multiply indefinitely after having lost the architrave that supported them, the invisibility that granted them their stamp of legitimacy. They promise safe guides and reassuring axiological horizons, but they are too close and thus tend to become blurry and quickly become obsolete.

Nevertheless, this does not stop the mechanism that set it into motion: in fact, it increases its speed. Schmitt was ultimately right when he said we are still in the Christian era: Its mechanisms, rusted by centuries of secularization, do not break down but creak along more or less ominously. Ultimately, we cannot do without the identity transmitted by the guiding image. In the dispersion of the global world, it is recalled intensely, summoned so that it moves ever closer, until it encases the body itself. The aestheticized universe in which we live develops in the Babel of guiding images – where heads of state are endowed with an aura that constantly calls them onto stage as if they were actors, and where actors freely share their judgments about the world and politics as if they were heads of state. And this universe is by no means solely one of manipulation. On the contrary: It is a universe in which the powers of recognition and of self-recognition are powerfully active; in fact, they dominate it.[48] It is the requirement of legitimacy and of self-recognition that moves the society of the image, constituting a demand so powerful it reveals how intense and engaging the anthropological foundation of this economy is – the intense need of the self that arrives from the most diverse latitudes. The society of the image cannot be reduced to manipulation and systematic ideological counterfeiting; it is more than ever the age guided by the most anxious need for authenticity and of knowing oneself that has perhaps ever appeared in history, and this produces all the critical elements that we attribute to it.

Populist leaders live within this ambiguity without resolving it or rendering it object and subject of a permanent crisis, of a permanent *Ausnahmezustand*. But since the crisis is permanent, it multiplies the demands for founding images; therefore, the imaginary must be fed with increasing intensity.[49] From the point of view of a formulation of a proposal in a political-aesthetic key, the idea and the possibility of a politics of the world's re-enchantment appears, to which we will turn our attention at the end of this book. Such a world would be a thoughtful and conscious renaming or, if one prefers, remythicization of the world that discovers new and renewed identities and narratives. The flourishing of identities forwards this homeopathic petition by highlighting how impractical it is, also in view of the finality for which it was generated, the Weberian "disenchantment of the world," the idea of an anonymous functionality that does not bear the mark of the hand that created it.

6

The Aesthetics of "The Withholding Power"

Unstable Power

What begins to take shape is not so much a definitive end, but something more akin to a long suffering, almost like a chronic state of illness. The general picture informs us of a constitutively unstable power, constantly exposed to the "state of exception," which stands on the basis of a dynamical-conflictual structure. We have said that the legitimacy of power is defined, in the Christian world, thanks to its capacity to be validated by its own supra-sensible foundation, to produce an imperishable representation of its own self that is tied to the transient one.[1] This is an aesthetic legitimization of power, in the sense that it travels through a reverberation, a self-representation that sanctions upstream what happens downstream. By retracing the trinitarian process, the sovereign, without being the vicar of the Son, discovers he possesses a Christological prerogative as the lord of this world.

The relative but systematic instability and *dynamis*, whose traces remain in the structure of power, are therefore tied to the remote (yet successful) contact between the principle and its hypostases, the real foundation of every legitimacy. If the relation fails, it falls into a sort of void in which anyone can get ahead. We are able to say that we are dealing with a structuring of power that, by way of its dynamic nature, is intimately exposed to instability and thus to exceptionality. If the correct relation between its various moments falls apart, the legitimacy of this form of power will go into crisis and the legitimate sovereign will no longer be distinguishable from the imposter, or to use the language of St. Paul, from the lookalike who embodies the *mysterium inquitatis*. It is a form of power that is linked to transcendent symbols and, at the same time, is organized around the symbols of transcendence.

Transcendence, among other things, can sometimes become immanent without losing its status. This is, for example – as was already said – the case of Charlemagne, *the swimming sovereign*, in Horst Bredekamp's words. Thanks to his majestic character, and by gathering sons, optimists, and the royal guard itself around him in the waters of the pool at Aachen, Charlemagne exercised an *embedded* power, connected to his powerful physical form, which dominated those who encircled him.[2] This is therefore a power that is always tied to economic cycles and thus unstable, especially when it is compared to the Eastern theocracies, as it is connected to an unstable relation and to the body and person of the sovereign. Since its inception, Western power appears to be restless and its sanction unstable. But this is not necessarily a detriment. This unstable, conflictual, and dynamic structure only needs stable symbols to validate it, symbols that attend to the restlessness surrounding it (such as when the moment of military victory transitions to the stable exercise of power).[3] The *katechon* is articulated even in an aesthetic symbology where the forms of power are universalized symbolically.

What does "transcendence" mean in this context? The transcendence of the universal assumes a different aspect with respect to what we expect in a certain religious lexicon. We must not look vertically but horizontally at what stands before us. The *katechonic* symbols are universal only insofar as they hold the gazes that originate from different angles into a single *facies*. In other terms, the perspective does not modify the consistency of the symbolic structure. This is the original cell of modern pluralism, a cell that becomes ill and suffers a process of decline. The *katechon* indicates a formal dynamic as meaningful as ever, which demonstrates that our worldly power is *constitutively* endowed with an unstable structure, and that crisis, the "state of exception," is co-essential with it. It holds and gives form to evil: By coming into contact with it, it paradoxically obstructs what emerges in its exanthematous and openly pathological dimension. Evil (which in this case is understood primarily as entropy) is precisely that and can be defeated only if it first shows itself.

Aesthetics and Politics after the *Katechon*

All of this has noticeable consequences on the aesthetic level, in particular from the point of view of four cardinal concepts in the history of the discipline. These are a) kitsch; b) prestige; c) the lookalike or double, as was already pointed out by the passage in Paul's Second Letter to the Thessalonians; and finally, d) the ruins of the future. It is an event that must also and above all be seen in the perspective of our present. To put it very and perhaps too peremptorily, the *katechon* is what we are missing today (rightly or not is hardly the issue here). We are the epoch that no longer recognizes the withholding power, the epoch that lives in an immense crisis of legitimization and self-legitimization. We have moved from the ancient to the modern to the postmodern and now to the Anthropocene, the entropic epoch par excellence.[4] As Peter Sloterdijk has clearly seen, it is characterized by its own aesthetic which swings it toward a fifth keyword: re-enchantment.[5]

The question is political, or rather aesthetical-political, and it can be summarized in the following choice: whether the crisis of legitimacy, that is, of the forms of the self-representation of power today, depends on a seismic shift that leads it – to state it generally – outside and beyond the symbolic system of Western Christianity, or whether this crisis instead sits precisely at the heart of this very system. From this latter point of view, we will not face a traumatic event but rather something that has been in the works for centuries. And that changes the perspective and the optics of the gaze. In this context, reconstructing a history of the *katechon* in relation to its "apocalyptic" and truly revelatory outcome, means questioning oneself about the present in an essential way. A present which, moreover, takes on strange and singular features, in many ways characteristic of the *hysteron proteron*, of the inversion of the last with the first recalled from the prologue of the Gospel of John.[6]

The inversion of the last with the first regards, above all, the outline of a development that runs, to recall the title of Tönnies famous book, from community to society.[7] The late modern universe and the global world would seem to have initiated a journey in the opposite direction, from society to community. No one is saying that this is necessarily a regression. But regardless of what has been said, it seems in any case difficult to deny that the global world has produced a sort of reversal with respect to the idea that the journey of secularization and modernity would have travelled from organic aggregation to the articulation of social life. A return to community is indeed obvious, as was said above, precisely in the mediated and global universe that produces, for example, greater numbers of subjects who are passionate about something that unites them, like a common bond or shared symbol.

Such a symbol lives by its own narrative extension, to invoke Paul Ricoeur.[8] In this framework a great example is the case of zero kilometre food, where we are really dealing with a transfer among very different spheres of the sensible, a sort of synesthetic miracle, where the first course is narrative, while the second, which occurs on the palate, integrates the first aspect into the scope of a small sacrificial rite, in which one destroys what was loved and cultivated by renewing the cyclical time of the festival and ancestral memory within the universe of linear and progressive time. The question of food is particularly symptomatic and important, much more than it would seem at first glance: It shows that the new community lives by required images, which create its identity. An identity that is at first narrative and then *embedded*. The identification thus happens in the simplest and most immediate way, through *embodiment*. Taste thus determines the features, however provisional they may be, of a community that lives and feeds on images, understood in a broad sense as a food even before food itself – a community that feeds on the icons that give it shape and keep it united and connected. It is as if we were dealing with forms of secular resacralization, almost with a secular reinterpretation of the eucharist, which would seem to refer to the *katechon*, to the lost bond of the community. It is the ritual of a community that both ritually and performatively – therefore also in a necessarily innovative way – returns to its own founding symbols.

Even on the basis of these considerations, one could say that the appearance in our time of an increasingly intense meaning of aestheticization also depends on a crisis of the *katechon*, which has not, however, renounced its own prerogatives in the society of the image, as confirmed by the fact that its absence demands and at the same time produces new symbolic replacements. One could in fact affirm that the phantasmatic presence of the *katechon* is ever more imminent. It continues to produce symbols, identities, and identifications which are apparently universal and, in reality, always more singular – even idiosyncratic and *embedded* – and connected to the body itself. Here in the world of the fall of the elites we find the final inheritance of the *katechon*, by now opened and fallen to the point of becoming a neurotic movement in which the requirement of legitimization coincides with a new turn upwards. Truly the power of the sacred – to say it with Hans Joas – floats around our heads, disturbing like a call that is unclear but difficult to tune out.[9]

Kitsch

In this context the dimension of kitsch undoubtedly plays a fundamental role: It constitutes from our point of view the most important aesthetic characteristic of the *katechon*. What is kitsch, ultimately, if not the attempt to realize a sort of "mass evocation" of the archetype? In this sense kitsch does not constitute – as Hermann Broch holds – a criminal addiction built on its fleeting aspect, that is too accommodating to widespread taste, but on the contrary embodies a widespread need in a way that is at times clever and at other times awkward. From its inception (and also in Broch) kitsch responds to a need for identity. It conflicts with the need for authenticity, since it wants to plant the idea that authenticity can be obtained on the cheap. Already in Norbert Elias's "The Kitsch Style and the Age of Kitsch" one can see this dialectic at work: Kitsch represents the expression of a society that works, or we might say a society of the market; it heralds the encounter between a true spiritual necessity and a satisfaction that instead is inauthentic and surrogated.[10] To formulate the question in still different terms, kitsch refers to an assigned identity, one placed in opposition to an authentic one passed down through the established canon of tradition. The question that is not asked and that instead ought to be posed in this context is if an assigned identity is really a false one. What kitsch highlights is that modernity produces an esoteric archetype, one easily consumed and thus distinct from the originary archetype, which is invisible and inaccessible. It would be Karl Kraus who remembers that kitsch provides something that true art cannot confer: social gratification.[11] Deepening the discourse, it must be said that kitsch is guilty of assigning a fake identity to the subject, which it finds pleasing; this is contrary to what occurs with the ideal of authentic subjectivity, which is capable of developing and affirming itself in an independent and at times tortured way, and if need be, against everything and everyone.

Totally absent from this debate is a fundamental question: whether the fact of being at least partially given is constitutive of identity (as is, moreover, implicit in the idea of education, which Nietzsche relates precisely to take up the subtitle of his *Ecce homo*: "how to become who one truly is"). We are dealing with an insuperable element, which the critics of kitsch do not want to take into account when they suggest an ideal of autonomy that is ultimately unsustainable, refuted as it is by concrete existence and the global diffusion of kitsch. In reality, kitsch allows something powerfully universal to flourish, namely, the fact that individuals need to be narrated, to discover themselves in semi-mythological micro-stories that function precisely as assignments of identity; to give life to places that are in some way comforting, also thanks to bad taste, as they favour the idea of feeling at home, or in other terms, the self-recognition of the subject.

To express it in even clearer terms: The subject needs a mythological transcendental, an easily accessed archetype that is always created anew. In many ways, therefore, kitsch is unavoidable and perhaps always a bit unseemly. From a historical point of view this dialectic is developed further in the works of Dwight Macdonald,[12] where kitsch takes on (albeit critically) a positive dimension. In its popular characterization, kitsch refers to the idea of a democratic, participatory, and shared art. Why does it happen? On closer inspection, it updates, within the precincts of bad taste, the dialectic of archetype and ectype; and it does it by exploiting in a casual way that generative reproducibility of contacts between different universes, of the wider and more democratic availability of products (cultural or not) evoked by Benjamin in the essay on *The Work of Art in the Age of its Technological Reproducibility*.

Through bad taste, art paradoxically regains full contact with life. And it does so by producing identifications beyond just an artistic level, obviously: The paradigm of all of this is, for Macdonald, the magazine *Life*, shared by both the upper and the middle class in a way that obscures their boundaries. Kitsch is transformed in this way: It no longer constitutes a derivative of high culture understood as authentic culture, but on the contrary introduces a corrosive element into the term "authenticity" that confuses its meanings (to take up Macdonald's argument and develop it in another direction). This signifies something fundamental, that is, fundamental in the sense of intensity: Identity is revealed as a powerful influence, which *almost like an archetype* comes before the process of identification rather than after it. Identity reveals, briefly, a performative power that strikes those who welcome it and share it to then become their *carte de visite*. In its profound structure, kitsch recaptures the dynamic and poietic identity of the *katechon*; it renews – or attempts to do so – the movement of the archetype by pivoting on its intensely performative and evocative nature.

Kitsch, therefore, is a culture that feeds on the difference between archetype and stereotype – thus confirming Leslie Fiedler's thesis in "The Middle Against Both Ends."[13] In other terms, in kitsch we find ourselves dealing with a late modern revival of the culture of the archetype, which preserves all its prerogatives as the generator of a community. But this is not all, even from the aesthetic point of view. We need to add the taste of the ruins, what kitsch confirms and contradicts by rekindling the feeling for "the small things of very bad taste" of Gozzanian memory. These second-order ruins – intimate rather than public, witnesses to an ancestral habit rather than an ethos – assume an involuntarily glamorous aspect that symbolically feeds the melancholic identity of our time.

By itself – it must be said – the difference between the archetype and the stereotype is not melancholic. Nevertheless, it becomes so, if one pays attention to the choice of the objects that today incarnate the archetype in the stereotype. Nothing is more significant in this regard than vintage; and certainly Slow Food also plays a role in this context. With vintage, we enter into a universe where we are even dressed evocatively in melancholy, which becomes the everyday outfit – an outfit with a touch of *glamour*, attractive and full of charm, like the past that will never return. Undoubtedly kitsch reintroduces the spirit of a community and in its way revives, so as to construct – as was already said – a system of recognition and self-recognition, a community that has its own symbols within a broader society understood as the hostile side from which it must be protected. This is connected to the mythical-ritual aspect permeating kitsch on many different levels, which deals with a real emerging of religious symbols or ones derived from pop culture – from sex to sport – newly ritualized through calls to loyalty or colours or to the flag, but also thanks to the grafting of spiritual traditions that activate itchy instincts, as the tantra does, where the ritualization of sex coincides with an increasingly widespread trend for all things *new age*.

Behind this characterization of kitsch one finds an aesthetics of everyday life that thoroughly permeates the forms of life and the identity of the subjects who are introduced into it.[14] Certainly, one could contest the idea that a public sporting event is an experience of kitsch; but that ultimately depends on a prejudice about kitsch rather than one about sporting events. If we were to define a sporting event as an experience for which the primary fundamental competence is finding communion with the object and its pervasive aura that stretches well beyond the original, things would be different. It is this and only this competence that defines the ability to realize the experience of kitsch. With this, the valuation of kitsch changes and kitsch reveals its most secret nature. It shows itself in its most proper quality as the more or less successful seed of an experience of the re-enchantment of the world. At the very peak of this ambiguity, where bad taste and the re-enchantment of the world paradoxically join together, the experience of kitsch is defined (or it might be better to say, it materializes). In this regard, the work of an artist like Jeff Koons is exemplary, whose *Balloon Venus* refers us to an archetypical experience whose aura transforms in ways both ironic and melancholic. Thanks to Koons the archetype also becomes kitsch and kitsch shows itself to be very close to the archetype, or rather, it reveals itself as such.

Edgar Morin has much to say to us about this topic (even though his discourse avoids any direct consideration of kitsch). In his essay "On Aesthetics,"[15] Morin notices that the necessity of an expression characterized aesthetically, that is, with no other purpose than to emanate its own splendour, not only runs through the entire course of human events, but also – at least at times – that of animals too. This is an ecstatic experience of a peculiar type, which places a shared, rather than solitary dimension at the centre of things, one capable of gathering and solidifying ever larger communities within itself. These communities are recognized within symbols that are not public, but private. In short, we are dealing with a paradoxical collective privatization of founding symbols, as witnessed even by the types of typically private, and at times even idiosyncratic, experiences and feelings (sex, sex symbols, the passion for a sporting idol). In this context how could we not be reminded of the mass cult of *followers*, for example of great heroes of soccer like Ronaldo or Messi, who are adored by tens of millions of fans?

A separate argument could be made for tattooing, which even ensures that the symbols remain on one's body, like a sort of heroic self-testimony cut into the skin. In this way, tattoos mark the signs of an identity that is both an affect and a creed intended to last until death. It is difficult to assess whether tattooing is kitsch. It is nevertheless in some way similar to kitsch, as it moves the archetype closer to its appreciator to the point that it is indistinguishable from the body. Even in the case of tattooing we are dealing with a claim to eternity, united, however, with the attempt to reduce the distance from the symbol, to tame its power. Kitsch domesticates the sacred, moving its signs and ritual practices closer to the subject, transgressing the limits of the *temenos* and introducing them into a private and domesticated space. It testifies to the will to make the sacred manageable, thus reducing the distance that keeps us subjugated (this is evident in certain miraculous objects of the 1950s and '60s, like the tiny fluorescent Madonna contained within a water-filled glass globe that, when shaken, makes it appear to be snowing). It is an attitude that not only concerns our own time, but also – as Salvatore Settis has shown without suggesting it as kitsch[16] – Renaissance art in its relation to antique art; for example, when ancient statues were reproduced with smaller dimensions than the originals so that they could be adapted to elite domestic settings and thus placed outside of the sacred precinct. Kitsch therefore produces a simple and brutal secularization, pointing to the need for portable symbols – symbols that have necessarily lost their relation to the invisible that belongs to the economy of the archetype.

The economy of kitsch still anticipates a relation between the invisible and the visible, one played as the memory of the *katechon* but on a different albeit parallel level. It presents a dialectic of loss and recovery that recalls the articulation of the trinitarian relation: how the Son must survive abandonment to achieve the promised salvation, which is successful precisely by reconnecting the broken thread. But this dialectic is interrupted. The unlikely recovery becomes impossible, and the disappearance of the Father labouriously reveals itself to be definitive, as was the case with Hamlet.[17] The disorientation is most profound; it is accompanied by the increasingly intense and challenging demands of symbols that are within reach, comforting, and readily available. Kitsch symbols are precisely what facilitate, at least apparently, the rediscovered harmony of the figures – albeit in an artificial form. It is a harmony that has become a mute yet powerful evocation, mindful of its origin. The privatized symbol bears an intense, sensible significance; and yet in the end it remains mute or assumes bizarre and distracting meanings. It is precisely, in this final case, kitsch.

This is an uncertain but powerful dialectic, in which the archetype that should be dissolved continues to act secretly and under false pretenses – or rather, false equivalencies. In fact, no one has ever really denied its necessity; nevertheless, it becomes partially opaque, losing its still relative transparency and its power, the seal of its legitimacy. Kitsch, from this point of view, reveals that it is a powerful category, based on what Adorno had already seen as its real value in the formation of identity.[18] Adorno was also making the needed distinctions between good kitsch and a kitsch that is no less good but less functional with respect to the formation of identity, and thus less kitsch. Kitsch possesses the power of nostalgia. At least from this point of view, insofar as it solidifies and expresses the intense desire to really feel at home wherever one lives, kitsch cannot be rejected as an abusive element of our real and imagined landscape, simply relegating it to the sphere of what lacks *politesse* or what is guilty of bad taste. In short, the dialectic of self-recognition emerges in kitsch. The absolute question: *Who am I, who are you?* – posed in Gadamer's book dedicated to Paul Celan – resonates here with great intensity.[19] Kitsch is ultimately a vain but very intense attempt to once again approach the relation to the origin, to resuscitate – albeit according to secularized and eccentric models – the dynamic of that trinitarian dialectic that, as we have seen, remains in force throughout the entire history of the *katechon*.

By taking one more step, one can say, in light of the previous considerations, that what falls into crisis is the symbolic economy of the moderne, with all of its emphasis on self-confirmation; and, along with it, the mode of production that still depends on it and that partly defined the physiognomy of this "new" time. On second thought, in fact, the capitalist economy is born from a meditated error regarding symbolic exchange, by which the investor is exposed to and undergoes – paying heed to the trinitarian framework understood in a symbolic-metaphoric and not a theological sense – a hemorrhagic event. In other terms, Jesus's sacrifice presupposes the salvation, which nevertheless must still come and thus looms in a future that could arrive tomorrow or be thousands of years away. In this way, there exists an organized disorder, a functional imbalance always on the hunt for compensation, for a healthy bleeding, and in short, for the oxymoronic state of a vital entropy. This is how one approaches the problem of dynamic forms – the types of forms that are open and not protected from time and death but ready to introject the new and make it a creative motif. These are *forme formanti* (forming forms), to use terminology from Luigi Pareyson's *Estetica* – forms that are in constant formation. The paradox of the entropic messiah still grounds our modernity: It is an order-disorder strategically structured on a deliberate loss of energy, which is subsequently restored. Today we are still dealing with – on a level that is functional and symbolic and not theological – a form of the divine conceived according to the model where one chooses a loss of energy while waiting for future compensation. This type of archetype progressively loses its power and falls silent.

The archetype is silent when the dialectic that stabilized it on the level of the economy of the image fails. In the dialectic between Father and Son, crossed by the Spirit, a historical dialectic is articulated that grounds messianic teleology. In other words, the imbalance, to reiterate what I was saying above, is revealed to be a motivating force that structures the messianic and therefore teleological orientation. The earthly figure is supported and justified in its mortal disguise by the intransient hypostasis that descends to its same level and thereby supports it and invites it to be together. It is a long journey that leads us to today, to our history. We now live without archetypes, evoking them with every turn of a world we no longer recognize. The archetype, as was said, has become blind and opaque; but, this obscurity highlights the call back to the origin. In this way it does not cease to perform its role as a model. We do not live in an age where it no longer exists, but in a time where it maintains its functionality without agreeing to step into its own grave; and this is not a recent development, but a long-term phenomenon that has slowly increased its significance and has endured at least since the Shakespearian crisis of sovereignty interpreted by Carl Schmitt.[20]

Modernity is thus dominated by its chthonic background as if by an abyss. However, the Freudian discovery of the unconscious is nothing other than this: the discovery that the subject has sunk to the bottom along with the archetype who supported it. It has lost its legitimacy. The unconscious is born as the individual unconscious, neurotic and irate, within the blinded archetype. And the individual unconscious is nothing other than, from this point of view, a derivative of the loss of contact with the collective one. If it were not once collective, the unconscious would simply be preconsciousness, something that is about to appear on the threshold of consciousness but that is almost consciously removed. In this very framework Jung's words from *The Archetypes of the Collective Unconscious* make sense, where one recalls the founding, potentially insidious, and reactive nature of the symbolic loss entrusted to common symbols: "Anyone who has lost the historical symbols and cannot be satisfied with substitutes is certainly in a very difficult position today: before him there yawns the void, and he turns away from it in horror."[21]

Yet Another Step: Hamlet and After

Hamlet's nocturnal conversation with the ghost of his father serves as a counterpart to the beheading of Louis XVI and foreshadows it. The king can be beheaded only if the dialogue with the invisible has broken down. The dynamic intensity of the modern, which is also and eminently kitsch, is both the sign and the symptom of the reckless search for a reissue of the foundation, of the apparently obsolete but, in reality, peremptory necessity of its re-flourishing.

What are the consequences? Once again the market tracks the modifications of the symbolic and brings them up to date. Today's age is dominated by a new market that is overrun with nostalgia. The despair over the loss of foundation creates infinite substitutes for the *katechon*, of the power that withholds and stabilizes, thanks to its symbols, institutions, and desires. This is the crisis of our time, which Massimo Cacciari diagnosed over forty years ago in *Krisis* – a crisis that involves and uproots the messianic identity of the modern. It can be confronted, whether from the epistemological point of view or from a political one, only by making reference to this messianic identity that has grown dim. It is the order of the nomos to be assailed by this crisis of the invisible, its paradoxical as ever disappearance which creates monsters: disoriented and nameless leaders with artificial and unreal bodies, like the Berlusconi of Paolo Sorrentino, blinded by ambition to gain access to that invisible which cannot (any longer) be accessed, that sinks into its own shadow always more artificial and marked by transience; *eidola* that – like Alba, the fluorescent rabbit by Eduardo Kac – emanate a light from their insides because they cannot receive it from heaven, which has denied them its gaze.

It might seem paradoxical but this is how it is: The messianic mechanism is completely internal to the secular identity of Western power, to its structures of meaning. One can even add that, in the absence of messianism, there is no legitimate politics, and that legitimate power is always a messianic power. On these bases, the current crisis finds motivations that allow it to be better identified, to comprehend the desolate panorama populated by crude and forgetful secularisms and by actually criminal populisms which lack any legitimacy. The globalized world – the universe of Marc Augé's *non-places*, which engulf us in the abyss of dispersion and anonymity – has, as we saw above, an intense inclination toward kitsch, and the easy rediscovery of the familiar homeland, each of us an Odysseus returning to Ithaca without the need to endure a long journey. The question of self-recognition, the dialectic of identity lost and won back, as we saw through kitsch, tries on familiar guises to renew the relation with the invisible foundation once proposed by the *katechon*. All of this is undoubtedly facilitated by technological reproducibility, which allows the transcendental-affective object – through which we recognize each other or hope to be recognized – to be available to everyone.

Nothing New

It is obvious that in the nineteenth century, and certainly during Italy's Risorgimento, all of this was already conceived in a rather clear way. The Romantic call for a new mythology, which arose from the bosom of subjectivity (as Friedrich Schlegel claims),[22] reveals the need to rediscover common symbols in a totally new way. From afar it recalls kitsch, at times demonstrated by the paintings of the Nazarene movement, which had wanted to renew the tradition of religious art and recall the invisible during a time which had already been completely secularized:[23] New forms of transcendence were invented by thinking about how to renew the ancient ones.

New mythologies are also narrations that identify a new people by taking them under their wing. In all of these cases, the exposure to kitsch is unavoidable, a risk that must ultimately be faced courageously – as Manzoni surely knows given the easy, rhythmic, and melodic attack of his "Marzo 1821" (March 1821). This was also known by the painters of Italian Romanticism when they proposed the mythologemes for the new Italy, choosing neither Zeus nor Aphrodite but instead the unnamed or the Garibaldian epic. In all of these cases it is obvious the artist understood the risk of producing kitsch; a challenge nevertheless faced with a determination and a courage matched only by the significance of the unscripted undertaking that the artist was carrying out: creating a new world of symbols that ensured for the members of a new populace the quality of being recognized as subjects descended from a common origin and recognizable in a shared lineage that is easy to access. They are reinventions of their origins, neither more nor less.

To accomplish this one must fearlessly risk becoming *grossier* or even kitsch. The nineteenth-century monument, for example the magnificent statue of Conte Verde by Pelagio Palagi in the Piazza Palazzo di Città in Turin, is an example of how they placed entirely discursive and narrative symbols, such as the victory of Amedeo VI of Savoy over the Turks, in the real and symbolic centre of the capital city. The statue, an eloquent symbol of legitimate power and the protection of a royal dynasty from an invader and enemy, is in a certain sense the living negation of Lessing's *Laocoonte*. We are in fact dealing with an eloquent, rather than a silent, hero par excellence like Laocoonte: with a symbol that guides us and shows us the way. A narrative symbol, moreover, that almost performs a *downgrade*, in the direction of a much more miserable time; almost an anticipation of the painting that narrates the chronicles of a life, often anything but glorious, as happens with the Pio Albergo Trivulzio by Morbelli, who reproduced it on multiple occasions beginning in the 1880s. They are "illustrative" works that recall a newspaper caption, a narrative extension, that in certain ways seem destined for *La Domenica del Corriere* (which began in 1899).

These are works that early on had to rely on technological reproducibility to really make their symbols – which were high and low – accessible: making their glamorous or contrite charms available to many and sharing in the pain of others. In this way kitsch, traced back to its problematic roots, restores one of the most significant specific qualities inherent in its being and in its concept: By its nature, it becomes ever more popular and available. The boundaries between popular art and democratic art are, obviously, both ambiguous and subtle. In this way we are inevitably led to face the art-democracy connection. The exchange between *high and low*, to repeat the fierce terms of the critique of Warhol, does not lead in the direction of an evangelical or democratic revolution of roles, but rather toward a sort of overlapping which arrives at the most confusing of pot-pourri, such as *We (all) Are the People* (which was, among other things, the title of the exhibition *Documenta 14* of 2017 which showed from 8 April to 16 July 2017 in Athens, and 10 June to 17 September 2017 in Kassel). It is an absolute revolution, or at least a subversion of the symbolic, which is realized through a sort of general lowering and relaxation of symbols, which lose their transcendent quality/localization and gradually become immanent. Pedro Almodóvar is perhaps the supreme teacher of this entire process.[24]

The Re-enchantment of the World

The decline of the symbolic is a process that does not make its order any less cogent, but simply incarnates it and exposes it to all of the variants connected to *embodiment*, to personalization, and to the arbitrary end of a value. Precisely in this framework, from the political point of view, the image of the body of the leader emerges,[25] which becomes a symbolic body, in its way restlessly and insistently kitsch (as confirmed by the figure of a Berlusconi already embalmed and ready to be displayed at Madame Tussaud's). It is increasingly necessary – as Marco Belpoliti says – to deepen the symbolic meaning of social phenomena. This, Belpoliti still claims, depends on the fact that power appeals to transcendent resources and structures that, by running out and breaking down, are incarnated in the very body of the sovereign through the simultaneously ridiculous and desperate attempt to universalize it. The ultimate figure of the symbology of power is, in the end, kitsch. This is the final step in the nostalgic dissolution of the *katechon*, which is consumed aesthetically and very melancholically. But it is perhaps also the overcoming of the *katechon* itself, since it goes beyond that step when at the centre of its event transcendence is recalled and its symbols disappear – what Roberto Esposito calls the "the machine of political theology."[26]

Let's try to better understand kitsch and its strategies. There is always something beyond kitsch, since it does not want to be what it is but wishes instead to be completely authentic. Kitsch orients us toward the restoration of a lost world: It is an aborted form of re-enchantment. Kitsch evokes the authentic foundations to the point of wanting to take their place, and in this way renews a heaven that has been emptied of the *katechon*; on the other hand, kitsch vaguely suggests and almost incarnates the *mysterium inquietatis* of Paul, evoking an exchange between the artificial and the authentic, all connected to the *glamour* that emanates from the authentic itself and that transforms or would like to transform the beast into a beauty.

Kitsch is revealed to be, in this light, more of a political than an aesthetic issue. The re-enchantment of the world becomes, from this point of view, an aesthetic-political constellation that derives from the melancholic decline of the *katechon* into kitsch. The late-modern universe needs a new symbolic bond, even if it is technologically mediated. The project of the re-enchantment of the world, which is evoked from many quarters, must not be misunderstood as a project for the respiritualization of the world, as it was conceived by Bernard Stiegler.[27] This is not a matter – as is rather obvious – of proposing an injection of spirituality into the secular world; rather, it is a matter of exploiting the energies that were introduced to it beginning with the disintegration of the yesterday's world in order to grant them a new status. The turn or the decline toward aesthetic capitalism – which is the true premise of what was defined as the aestheticization of the world – is understood as compensatory, as compensation for something that was lost; and above all ne must understand what truly has been lost. It is the persistence of the political-social bond, the self-representation of the collective self that was guaranteed by the juridical form of the *katechon*. In other terms, the symbolic system which allowed for society's self-recognition falls into crisis.

These symbols are both individual and collective forms of self-recognition. What matters here is identity as *civitas* and society. Not surprisingly, Carl Schmitt had identified nihilism with the crisis of the *katechon*.[28] Nihilism is the melancholic identity that was discussed above; yet, it is completely different than a sterile or unproductive identity. On the contrary, it unleashes a liberation of energies connected to the desire to re-establish the small ancient world that immediately becomes a small modern world intensely networked by technologies and ravenous in its desirous identity. Burdened by a corrosive anxiety and in search of a universal identity, desire cannot, by its very nature, avoid individualizing it, and therefore leaves its experiment unsatisfied and, moreover, feels condemned to repeat it all over again to create thousands and thousands of diverse instances of the collective self. We are thus dealing with an infinite number of models.

Moreover, desire understands its (imaginary) object as *glamorous* and enchanting: It is the image that matters. This desire is, therefore, by its nature, particular: It is satisfied and embodied not in the object but in the image. This is what confers primary value, identity, authenticity, the certainty of being who we are in the reflection of the other that now becomes our own guise. In other terms, the image is the true object of desire and not simply its medium. This radically changes the nature of satisfaction, which is not at all a replacement but entirely realized in reference to the image and to its *embodiment*. The images (at least these images) are completely tied to the market, which has its own foundation and psycho-anthropological outcome, its own qualitative characteristic, as its goods are directed toward each individual (who becomes such through goods) and not toward the anonymous masses. The qualitative aspect *of* goods therefore takes centre stage through a series of predicates that refer to the mirror of authenticity and uniqueness, to an auratic quality. Slow Food is exemplary in this regard: Food reverberates with the identity of a specific place and of those who dwell there (and even more so of those who once dwelled there). The taste of food is its story, and tasting is above all mythical. Thus, it is the market that approximates art, much more than art resembles the market. The aura of goods, the real motor of the market, functions not only with luxury objects where it is always the case: In this regard the weekend supplement of the *Financial Times* is exemplary, which increasingly refers to a comingling of luxury and the *green economy* that are combined and mutually benefit each other, and along the way create objects that reflect a rather unified taste.

In this context the Marxian notion of exchange value infinitely succumbs not to use value but to the auratic importance of objects, whereby values such as the authentic and the immutable are axiologically given centre stage. What is unique and immutable becomes the central and perhaps supreme demand of the market; and it is, in reality, an aesthetic power, an auratic value that is spread out over goods and that seems to modify – if not contradict – the thesis Benjamin proposes in *The Work of Art in the Age of its Technological Reproducibility*. And so another strength appears, which is not the diffuse aestheticization of the world but rather its opposite, the auratic nature of the object. It is not the aesthetic universe that has been spread out over the world and subjugated it: it is instead the object, unique in its iterations, that returns to radiate its sacred aura of the past across the globalized world – an aura that belongs to what is unique and unrepeatable. The unique and the unrepeatable are the true desiderata of the market, thus disposed to reproduce the ineffable object infinitely. The aura anticipates economic value and refers to the desire to be recognized, the dramatic acknowledgment within a world that in many respects is barely livable, obscure, and cloudy.

Could we translate the question into other terms and make the point of view presented here a bit more precise? If so, we would then say that we exist in a world where (taking up a theme dear to Giuliana Bruno) emotions become spatialized and transformed into atmospheres.[29] Here one can also speak of a melancholic identity, precisely because the desires that belong to identities are put into play and expressed through images that are always images of itself, reflected images. This is how the miracle happens: The image itself constitutes a compensatory form of capital able to overturn the melancholic and thus entropic tendency. Productively diffractive in the assignment of energies, it transforms the tendency into a projectual *framework*. In fact, the images project identities and thus ways of being.

An archetypical compensation is presented today as the true background not only for the market of art and of antiques, but also and ultimately for the goods that are sold at the supermarket, where, for example, certifications of environmental responsibility are increasingly important. Identity, in this sequence, signifies authenticity, and authenticity first and foremost signifies rootedness and localization. That means that goods always have an identity qualified through images, in the sense that they acquire an atmospheric and almost ubiquitous identity, thus making their aura palpable. We are dealing with a revolution of feeling, and thus of feelings, whose significance and importance are not easily overestimated. Feeling is no longer a private issue; it is no longer idiosyncratic and in fact even becomes democratic. A vast array of subjects participates and shares the experience to the degree that they belong to the same place, or rather, to the same symbolic topology. These are subjects who characterize and create the place insofar as they recognize its atmosphere and, by participating in it, create it. To express it in other terms, the feeling is spatialized. The atmosphere becomes something similar to the agora, the public space in which a *communis opinio* is generated, the premise of a new democracy that is installed in the *polis* restricted to the community of participants. Premise, in this case, means that which is truly shared.

From this point of view the atmosphere is a sort of necessary hermeneutical and dialogical premise. Art plays a founding role in this context. In this regard, many of Ólafur Elíasson's works are quite eloquent, such as *Weather Project*, the AROS Aarhus Art Museum in Denmark, or the more recent work at the Palace of Versailles. In all of these examples, light dominates, encompassing the environments and the individuals, now becoming tridimensional by going beyond the two dimensions of the canvas or in any case of the flat surface. The light in these contexts performs the role of an atmospheric transcendental, inviting us to stay in a determinate climate: It involves everyone and says to everyone which place this is and where we are as individuals and as a group. It slows down the pace of life and of the gaze, compelling us to linger on ourselves and on what encircles us. In short, it creates identity and generates community, as the *Weather Project* (2004) attests – the sun of Elíasson that shines in the Tate Modern, under which people meet, walk, or simply lay down to enjoy the particular atmosphere, perhaps taking advantage of an unexpected tan. The same goes for the galleria that stands above the Aarhus Art Museum, where the public lives in a real environment separated from the rest of the world, a community dedicated only to those who, at the final level, cross the luminous rainbow.

The atmosphere exteriorizes and spatializes the interior sphere of feeling; we could say that it expresses a political-therapeutic vocation. The atmosphere makes feelings – as intuitable – public, which are thus transferred in a sphere not prescribed for it, and ultimately almost entirely experimental: By exteriorizing feeling, by participating in it, it escapes from the *temenos* of ineffable interiority, restores it to the public space from which modernity and modern life have essentially excluded it, except for those zones assigned to "public sentiment," where it was nonetheless always subtracted from daily life. This is the case of the theatre or of the large collective manifestation of sport or politics, in which feeling is more or less emphatically shared by many people or even by a mass of them. In any case, this has nothing to do with the massive crowds that are sadly commonplace with almost all dictators. The atmospheric feeling must not be confused with these types of demonstrations, where feeling would be converted into an ecstatic feeling, impacting the individual will by voiding it in the collective one.[30] In shared atmospheres (like those created by Elíasson) subjects once again feel themselves in others and others in themselves, based not on an abuse of the self's power but by virtue of a common vital and technological humus that joins one to the other.

Often, through the fundamental mediation of a technological medium, the involved subjects begin again to connect physical feeling (to be clear, what is transmitted by the senses) with the dimension of interior feeling: In other terms, they renew the bonds that were severed in the Christian-modern world between sensibility and the interior realm. This produces a subjectivity that is steadier and more integrated with the world, more rooted, in both its physical and interior forms. In this way the connection between human life and animal and even vegetal nature is exalted: Not surprisingly, the theme of the life of plants is currently having a moment in philosophy. This interest expressed by a good deal of contemporary philosophy leads us into zones theoretically (and in every sense) particularly sensible,[31] in which feeling is moved closer to physical and cultural roots, and vice versa, as rooted, lymphatic feeling – to take up the direction of Nicolas Bourriaud regarding certain aspects of contemporary art.[32] The concept of aura is renewed when it is emancipated from the precinct of the sacred and expanded over the entire biotechnological ecosystem contemplated by the work of art.[33] That becomes particularly obvious, and even exemplary, in the case of public art, especially when it chooses light as its primary expressive vehicle.

This transition produces two fundamental modifications on the intimately connected levels of the aesthetic and the political. The classification of the figurative arts becomes increasingly uncertain and blurry:[34] Works of architecture, for example, can be made of light and colour, and thus become "atmospheric" by individualizing and characterizing the forms of life. Public art responds to the challenge which originates in the forms of life also harmed by a widespread and banal architectonic rationalism, that often builds without really constructing. The artistic mythopoeia immediately becomes political. The ancient vocation of art to give structure to the space that surrounds it – already emphasized by Heidegger in the example of the Greek temple – becomes much less utopian given the possibilities foreshadowed by media technologies. As we have seen, this is one of the traits that characterizes Elíasson's poetics, especially in his museum interventions.

The collective subject, which in this way grows into its own features, is no longer constituted as a sum of individuals who overcome their empirical caducity to elevate themselves to the powerful abstraction (based on Rousseau's constitutional model) of the sovereign body; rather, it occurs according to a sort of continuity we might call humoral, a climatic community whose only bond is taste and common feeling, which flourishes only in the negative. In short: "Whoever disagrees doesn't fit in!" Feeling is no longer interiorized, as was the tradition of the modern subject,[35] but is now lymphatic: It rediscovers and renews its own roots in a key that is not only psychological, but truly "vegetal," metaphorically and not. Feeling itself becomes a sort of ecological niche that surrounds our self with our own remains from a truly psychobiological past.[36] In the hallway of the Aarhus Art Museum, subjects are emancipated from the weight of individual identity in favour of a collective identity with atmospheric traits. Thus, we are not dealing with a mystical collective, or the adulating crowds belonging to twentieth-century totalitarianisms, but with a tender and much less binding link. This rooting and mythopoetic activity is most fully expressed by art. In the background a co-created utopia, only apparently regressive, takes shape: the *mass society* becomes a *constellation of community*, characterized by diverse symbolic and/or atmospheric identities.

In other terms, through these installations, we are dealing with the sign of a transition from society to community, in which public art plays the role of protagonist and drives the process toward an acceptable outcome, namely, providing "good" symbols within a habitable and unpolluted ecosystem of values that reinforces the organic bond of the community without making it exclusive.[37] We are dealing with an ethos that is and remains modern, and not a renewal of an ancient organic bond founded on blood.[38] It is as if in our world the private sphere were to ambiguously occupy the spaces, the prerogatives, and the meanings of the public one, giving rise to an infinity of diverse communities. There are a great many communitarian constellations that come to be in the global world, all connected with each other by a common passion or by an idiosyncrasy shared in the media. This marks a sharp loss of universality, accompanied by a sort of deeply problematic localization of values, and moreover, of truth itself.

It is, for example, rather difficult – to suggest a very dramatic argument – to enforce human values by leveraging their universal significance when the indignation (justified or not) faced by certain subjects is unleashed in way that is difficult to control. When forms of life are touched, the local takes the place of the universal, customs take the place of civil or penal codes, and the injured community rises up against the society guilty of all of the real or imaginary harms that it has suffered. Forms of life are politicized in an increasingly intense way[39] and thus become the vehicle and the fulcrum of many choices: Voting is a good example (think about how quality of life now factors greatly into political decisions). In this context, institutions take on an alien and alienating face that leads to something like Brexit, regardless of every objective reason against it. Symmetrically, nature returns to impose itself on society and culture, as we have been able to witness during the lockdown, when we were finally able to rediscover the colour of the sky. In our world, first nature is always wrapped around second nature, and in ways that are increasingly inescapable – for example Francesco Simeti's work at the Italian consulate in New York from 2020, or Stefano Boeri's Bosconavigli, where the surfaces of the design have walls that are literally covered in greenery. Even these ways of designing and making art respond to a precise and localized demand, one formulated by forms of human life that now ask to be protected.

The idea of the re-enchantment of the world also contains this: that one ought to design by following the anthropological need to bring the horizon closer, to mark off the borders of the community in order to create places where one can put down roots. The work of Ettore Spalletti also testifies to this, in which colour undergoes a transformation that turns it into light.[40] All of these aforementioned cases reveal the appreciation of the work of art is a non-thematic appreciation. This aspect is, in reality, a fundamental element of appreciation in general, especially in the figurative arts. In other terms, only in rare cases does the work really constitute a text, while more often it is configured as a sort of atmospheric context into which we are inserted, whether we experience the art in monumental environments and are occupied in activities that in no way deal with aesthetic contemplation, or when the work slips into the background after having been the object of our personal attention. Here arises a sort of immersive vocation of the figurative arts in their complexity (and architecture in particular). This occurs also due to the explicit intention of the author, with background music or soundtracks that function explicitly as the context of action. More generally, the contextual aspect of art is in force in the cases where the purpose of art is not obvious and remains in the background, as also happens with ornamental art, which discretely elevates the dignity of existence. To move to lesser examples, even the simple choice of where to go to enjoy an aperitivo or a coffee with an acquaintance or a friend depends ultimately on a choice in which the artistic and ornamental context plays its role. This is a very important and often overlooked issue, which is worthy of our attention precisely because the concretely socializing value of art emerges in it, which from time to time generates a community by granting them their own symbols. We are dealing with symbols endowed with a performative content of the highest order, or to invoke Horst Bredekamp's work, real image acts.[41]

What art puts forwards does not at all suggest, from this point of view, something unscripted, but rather a sort of constant task of art, an interweaving of motivations on which Salvatore Settis had recently attracted attention by relativizing the distance between the ancient, the modern, and the contemporary.[42] The magnificent *Door Tree-Cedar* by Penone, the subject of Settis's commentary, attests to a cultural evolution in which natural symbols constantly rescue the cultural ones, thus creating an itinerary between art, nature, and their symbols, that constantly generates new works. It is precisely this connection that accounts for the always contextual character of every art. When we speak of immersivity, we should therefore remember that it merely constitutes the beginning of every art. The relation between context and artistic text reverberates in different symbolic forms and broadly across history; its field is more originary, set into the relation art-nature. We confirm that every art, from this point of view, is immersive; it is a text that at any moment can become a context, but also the opposite.[43]

This dimension clouds the distinction between art and landscape, or rather between an aesthetics of art and an aesthetics of landscape, in a significant way. From both points of view aesthetic appreciation occurs not as thematic, but rather as athematic, as a given context that draws its focus on a text that is not necessarily aesthetic, but could instead be something common, like two friends meeting in a bar as we were saying earlier. This overturning of focal points is a real *bouleversement* of aesthetic appreciation as it is traditionally understood, according to which the sequence moves from the subject to the object, in a contemplative relation that is also a relation of power. Now the imaginary context instead constitutes (or can constitute) the principle, the imprinting, the coining of a new idea of public space that understands it as a powerfully synaptic symbolic space, lived in common but free from participation that is direct, thematic, and conscious of the subjects involved.[44] Obviously, this does not mean that we are dealing with an ideological environment or a space of manipulation. More precisely, we are not dealing with a lack of awareness but with an indirect awareness, in some way "diffused," as is the case when we perceive an atmosphere. The technologically immersive and virtual dimension therefore emphasizes how much is already "in nature." In this way it can contribute to the creation of community, but also pursue the propensity toward the community that the global world engenders with ever increasing intensity.

In this framework, the exchange between nature and culture (or rather, between nature and technics) becomes increasingly intense; and the idea emerges – which is at the same time a proposal – for a new organicity, almost neoclassical, of the technologically mediated social bond. From this point of view, before even talking about technology and adopting the perspective that follows, it would be worth asking: What are the issues that technology addresses? What are the desires that technology implants? If the bond between technology and desire has now become a central feature, it is thanks to the power of enchantment inherent to the way technology works. And so the idea, perhaps still prevalent, of technology as an anonymous process begins to wane.[45] Moreover, it is precisely this bond that exalts the idea of a purely technological definition of re-enchantment, which therefore does not betray its origins, as it has nothing to do with a contrasting relation between first and second nature, but rather with the integration of the two, so that the spell promised by the first can be unleashed from the second.

The ancient and classical connection par excellence between art and ethos returns to reveal itself in all of its power, as I endeavoured to show elsewhere by referring to the work of Andy Warhol, a proponent of a new ethos of late modernity that lives within the goods that constitute its great ornament.[46] The idea of an art that generates an ethos necessarily stands forth. The artistic symbols consciously return to become generative, to create a collectivity capable of renewing them poetically and not remaining in their own territory. It is as if art were to challenge the *temenos* each time by creating it, restoring it, and redefining its profile. Art, from this point of view – pardon the overly emphatic expression – restores the ethos of the *polis*, or at least helps to make it, innovating it with its own means. It operates on cultural memory by treating its wounds and proposing itself as its foundation. Undoubtedly, we have both a hypothesis and a project that return to validate, in their own way, the aspiration of the classical to an albeit perishable eternity. On this path, moreover, Hegel's thesis about "the end of art considered in its highest vocation" in the modern world is rejected, confronted with evidence that the classic endures in time – as Giovanni Gentile says[47] – by being romanticized in a sort of eternal cyclicality in which the melancholy for the lost myth is re-actualized again and again.

Insofar as art provides a new foundation for the identity of a collectivity, we are dealing with a narrative memory that grants a place and a history to the members of a community. Not surprisingly, we are surrounded by mytho-historical series that hearken back to the formation of our age like *The Lord of the Rings*, or with mythological narrations that concern the origin of modern Europe like *Knightfall* on Netflix. In other words, we are observing continuous high and low resurgences of what the Romantics defined as "new mythologies." It is a mythicizing of art and, at the same time, of art and of politics. But perhaps, on second glance, the true wager is the mythicizing of the *logos* in general.

The mythical compensation which occupied Jung can be understood etymologically in this context as a narrative development of the *logos*. But what does all of this have to do with the argument of this book? Perhaps it has more to do with the absence of the *katechon* than with its presence. What is constant today is not so much the looming presence of the *katechon* but its continual evocation, useful also for exorcising the nightmare of the end times and the reappearing image of a death that takes over life and engulfs it, as in Tiziano Sclavi's *Dylan Dog*.

It is a matter of renovating some of the founding discourses in the late-modern global world that maintain the characteristics of the *katechon* by pluralizing its narrations, taking advantage of the fact that this world constitutes in reality one itinerary through a thousand different villages, no one of which is truly autonomous from the others. The demand put forward by subjects – as we were saying – is for a common story that takes advantage of images and its narrative voice. The demand for images in our time, which we have interpreted as the demand for identity, finds one of its more accomplished responses in narrative images, which confer the coveted identity by creating personality types. This is precisely the secret of heroes in *comics* and a wide array of television series: a narrative fabric developed around character types who are devoid of psychological ripples, free from idiosyncrasies, and as such become optimal transmitters of the story. The characteristic of these personalities is precisely to function as a means for the actions that run through them. Attention is never directed on the characters, lest it be as a vertex or point of arrival for a narrative that crosses through them. In other terms, a collective narrative needs very stable characters who do not draw attention to their internal events and that places the focus on the adventure they are living. The comic strip is, from this point of view, exemplary, since none of its protagonists ever lose their almost epic stability. Just as Hector could not refuse to leave the Scaean Gates in response to Achilles's challenge, so too Donald Duck would no longer be himself if, for a moment, he were to become lucky. In this way, a narration of individual events becomes a shared narrative, as the characters are on the whole known and constant whether in terms of their possible actions and reactions, their passions, their abilities and shortcomings, and even their destiny: Here then arises a story that gathers individuals as a collective, that elicits a common empathic reaction that is not the same as the one elicited by, for example, the great bourgeoise novels where individual characters develop at the expense of the story. The psyches of Raskolnikov in *Crime and Punishment* or Frédéric Moreau in *Sentimental Education* add value to the history they are living or have lived and constitute the liveliest aspect of the narration.

The point, therefore, is that we all sense the need to be narrated, to recognize ourselves in a past, even if it is the most mythical and fantastic. This probably occurs because being narrated is an anthropological necessity: Everyone, each one of us, has the need for a common but also individual and fitting story, of being other-directed at least in part, especially in a universe that is too vast – but also too small – like the global one, thus giving chase to the variable nature of its subjects who constitute something like an archipelago or a mosaic. The global world remembers the archipelago or mosaic precisely to the degree that it is constituted by thousands of histories and stories that are woven together and overlap each other in the universe of mass media. The call back to organic and fusional identity is constant where it is a matter of real clubs of aficionados dedicated to this or that banner, insignia, brand, team, or even faith, etc. It is a story that scars the infinite nostalgia of not knowing who we are by doling out identities profusely in a market that always demands their release into a world that is hungry for them. The nostalgia for the lost *katechon* is translated into thousands of memories that nonetheless know, ideally, that the edges of the wound that they would like to sew shut should remain open. Identity, in the end, is never sated and needs to be fed constantly. Precisely through these open edges the market worms its way in, producing abundant identities through images. All of these images have a narrative extension. Every one of them contains a history that affects, influences, and encloses the subject by introducing it to a collective identity. Such an identity is always in need of integrations, additions, modifications, or even obsolescence so it can be replaced by others. We could say that the capitalistic world has, in some way, reacted to the disenchantment of the world that it had itself produced: It made it by capturing and integrating into itself the increasingly intense question of an albeit fictitious identity (but which one isn't?), and thus also of those identities derived from the *fictio*.

The saturated identity is therefore the principle of the market, and its saturation constitutes both an economic and a political risk. From the economic point of view, the saturation of identity would disrupt the production of identitarian goods, creating a monochromatic and monotonous market that does not know competition (as was said years ago about the Soviet economy). The thousands of identities produced by the market are the secularized forms of an identity that has theological ancestry, but this has nothing to do with theocracy. The opposite is in fact true. The saturated identity, produced by a myth that is likewise saturated, is – as we are well aware – the principle of all totalitarianisms, which are not guilty because they produce and draw upon mythology, but, on the contrary, are guilty because they draw upon it poorly or too little, referring to a single founding myth, thus blocking the mythical mythopoiesis in its pluralistic nature, destined to be multiplied in the thousands of stories that are the thousands and thousands of identities of this world, the infinite possible narrations that compete with the millions of men and women who populate a single land. Therefore, this does not require us to leave the society of the spectacle or extinguish the nostalgia for the *katechon*; rather, it is a matter of dwelling there in the proper manner. All of the identities belong to the imaginary, but not all of them are capable of promoting the life of those that share it with them. Therefore – to limit ourselves here to a summary and general suggestion – more than ever we need an ethics of the image and of imaginaries that provides a principle of prohibition against harmful identities: First among those is what was generically defined as saturated. But this will also mean admitting that democracies can be renewed by making recourse to new myths that are always new axiologies, new horizons for practice. Without remythicization, a push toward renewal of any type is unthinkable. The myths must be numerous (even if controlled), if one wants to rediscover the propulsive force that our century seems to have lost. The fear of the end – to once again take up what I attempted to say in the preceding pages – is replaced by the dread or the terror of facing the same, which is constantly projected as an almost inevitable end, as the one totalizing myth (at least as regards the explicit ones). This must be avoided.

What does all of this mean from the political and aesthetical-political point of view? It is first of all necessary to refute the idea that democracy and secularism or democracy and secularization function as the first principles of the discourse. In reality, democracy and pluralism do not function without an at least remotely theological, mythical, mythical-theological foundation. What secures a democracy and a good democracy is a mythical mythopoiesis that knows how to protect us from disturbing and violent symbols and how to favour those that are able to restore the drive and the energy toward the future. The ethics of the image to which it aspires would thus be an ecological ethics, capable of measuring the symbolic ecosystem based on its capacity to encourage life and its future. Certainly, these words can appear too simplistic. And yet, where the distinction between nature and culture has definitively collapsed (as has occurred today),[48] one must understand – also following Goethe's teachings – technological processes and the same technological progress in an ecological key that restores a cosmic breath to the human ecosystem. Every *techne* (and the current technology with unusual power) challenges humanity on the level of the poetic and productive exchange with nature.[49] Mythically and technologically rediscovering the cosmos constitutes the task for a future humanity that can reach beyond the present with a renewed passion.[50]

Notes

Introduction

1 On the archetypical presence of time see above all the first chapter of Ernst Bloch, *The Spirit of Utopia*, trans. Anthony A. Nassar (Stanford, CA: Stanford University Press, 2000).

2 See Piero Gobetti, "Un artista moderno: Felice Casorati," in *Opere complete*, vol. 2: *Scritti storici, letterari e filosofici*, ed. P. Spriano (Torino: Einaudi, 1969), 629. (The essay was originally included in *L'Ordine Nuovo* 19 June 1921.)

3 See Jacob Taubes, *Occidental Eschatology* (Stanford, CA: Stanford University Press, 2009).

4 For everything concerning this story, which here will be considered above all through the lens of its influence on the present, this book is indebted to its reconstruction in Francesca Monateri's *Katechon. Filosofia, politica, estetica* (Torino: Bollati Boringhieri, 2022).

5 Erik Peterson, *Die Kirche aus Juden und Heiden* (Verlag nicht ermittelbar, 1936).

6 See Monateri, *Katechon*, chap. 2, par. 5.

7 Permit me to refer the reader to my book, *L'archetipo cieco. Variazioni sull'individuo modern* (Torino: Rosenberg & Sellier, 2021).

8 Carl Schmitt, *Glossarium: Aufzeichnungen Aus Den Jahren 1947 Bis 1958* (Berlin: Duncker & Humblot, 2015), 61.

Chapter One

1 See Hans Joas, *The Power of the Sacred: An Alternative to the Narrative of Disenchantment* (Oxford, UK: Oxford University Press, 2021).

2 See Peppino Ortoleva, *Miti a bassa intensità. Racconti, media, vita quotidiana* (Torino: Einaudi, 2019).

3 On this topic see above all Gernot Böhme, *Critique of Aesthetic Capitalism* (Milan: Mimesis, 2017).

4 See Bruno Latour, *We Have Never Been Modern* (Cambridge, MA: Harvard University Press, 2012), and *Facing Gaia: Eight Lectures on the New Climatic Regime* (John Wiley & Sons, 2017).

5 On the debate over postmodernism and a fair accounting of its themes see Peter Carravetta, *Del postmoderno. Critica e cultura in America all'alba del Duemila* (Milan: Bompiani, 2009); Elio Franzini, *Moderno e postmoderno. Un bilancio* (Milan: Raffaello Cortina, 2018).

6 Francis Fukuyama, *The End of History and the Last Man* (New York: Simon and Schuster, 2006).

7 Robert Venturi, Denise Scott Brown, and Steven Izenour. *Learning from Las Vegas, Revised Edition: The Forgotten Symbolism of Architectural Form* (Boston, MA: MIT Press, 1977).

8 On this topic permit me to refer the reader to my essay "Caos e morfogenesi nel romanticismo tedesco," in *Morfologie del moderno. Saggi di ermeneutica dell'immagine* (Genova: Il Melangolo, 2006), 61–72.

9 On the messianic event and its meaning, see above all Taubes, *Occidental Eschatology*.

10 See Ernst Behler, *Unendliche Perfektibilität. Europäische Romantik und französische Revolution* (Paderborn-München: Schöningh, 1989).

11 On this see Jean-Pierre Dupuy, *Pour un catastrophisme éclairé. Quand l'impossible est certain* (Paris: Seuil, 2002).

12 Victor Ieronim Stoichita, *L'effet Sherlock Holmes: variations du regard de Manet à Hitchcock* (Paris: Hazan, 2015).

13 See Böhme, *Critique of Aesthetic Capitalism* (Milan: Mimesis International, 2017).

14 See Böhme's critique of Wolfgang Haug's *Warenästhetik* in *Critique of Aesthetic Capitalism* (Milan: Mimesis International, 2017): "Reconstructing Critical Theory," "Culture Industry and Aesthetic Economy," 15–17, 45.

15 On this point see Tonino Griffero, *Atmospheres: Aesthetics of Emotional Spaces* (London: Routledge, 2016); Tonino Griffero and Marco Tedeschini, *Atmosphere and Aesthetics: A Plural Perspective* (Springer Nature, 2019); Tonino Griffero, *The Atmospheric "We": Moods and Collective Feelings* (Milan: Mimesis International, 2021).

16 On this theme see Stefano Poggi, *Il colore e l'ombra. La Trasparenza da Aristotele a Cézanne* (Bologna: Il Mulino, 2019).

17 See O. Breidbach, K. Klinger, M. Müller, *Camera obscura. Die Dunkelkammer in ihrer historischen Entwicklung* (Stuttgart: F. Steiner, 2013), where it is revealed that the camera obscura requires all gazes to undergo the same focus.

18 See Marie-Josè Mondzain, *L'immagine che uccide. La violenza come spettacolo dalle Torri gemelle all'Isis*, Italian translation EDB (Bologna 2017); and, as regards the image/invisible relation which was formed in the Byzantine tradition, retaining an important meaning in the contemporary world, Mondzain, *Image, Icon, Economy: The Byzantine Origins of the Contemporary Imaginary* (Stanford, CA: Stanford University Press, 2005).

19 Mondzain, *Le Commerce des regards* (Paris: Editions du Seuil, 2009), 38. Regarding the "necessity of the invisible," see more recently Michele Guerra, *Il limite dello sguardo. Oltre i confini delle immagini* (Milano: Raffaello Cortina, 2020).

20 See Ernst Cassirer, *The Question of Jean-Jacques Rousseau* (Bloomington, IN: Indiana University Press, 1963).

21 As Horst Bredekamp also revealed in relation to the case of the centre of Berlin in *Berlin am Mittelmeer: kleine Architekturgeschichte der Sehnsucht nach dem Süden* (Verlag Klaus Wagenbach, 2018).

22 The nude represents an ideal that caused a stir and finds its importance in German classicism, from Goethe to Hegel, as an ancient text bears witness, that nonetheless remains meaningful and current, at least from this point of view, like that of W. Rehm, *Griechentum und Goethezeit. Geschichte eines Glaubens* (Bern: Francke, 1952).

23 Theodor Adorno, *The Jargon of Authenticity* (London: Routledge, 2013).

Chapter Two

1 The authenticity of this letter has been in doubt since the end of the 1700s. Cf. J.E.C. Schmidt, *Vermutungen über die beiden Briefen der Thessalonicher* (Hadamar, 1798). The debate over the authenticity of this text is also quite rich. Today noted scholars like Olivier Boulnois, *Saint Paul et la philosophie: Une introduction à l'essence du christianisme* (2022) tend to reject outright its authenticity, while less radical judgments can be found in the past, among which we will limit ourselves here to mention Ernest Best, *The First and Second Epistles to the Thessalonians* (New York: Harper and Row, 1972), 50, for which the non-authenticity of Thessalonians 2 does not appear evident, at least from a doctrinal point of view.

2 Quoted from *The New Oxford Annotated Bible with Apocrypha: New Revised Standard Version* (United Kingdom: Oxford University Press, 2010).

3 On this idea see the classic work by Otto Pöggler, *Hegels Kritik der Romantik* (Munich: Fink, 1999); also, eds. Claudio Ciancio and Federico Vercellone, *Romanticismo e modernità. Atti del Convegno (Torino 25–27 maggio 1995)* (Torino: Zamorani, 1997).

4 On this point, see above all Massimo Cacciari, *The Withholding Power: An Essay on Political* Theology, trans. Edi Pucci. (New York: Bloomsbury Publishing, 2018). From the point of view of a complete historical reconstruction of the question see Francesca Monateri, *Katechon. Filosofia, politica, estetica* (Torino: Bollati

Boringhieri, 2022). From a point of view that grants a centrality to politics that does not depend on the *katechon* there is instead Roberto Esposito, *Two: The Machine of Political Theology and the Place of Thought* (New York: Fordham University Press, 2015), which is followed by his *Politics and Negation: For an Affirmative Philosophy* (Cambridge, UK: Polity Press, 2019); and *Institution* (Cambridge, UK: Polity Press, 2019).

5 Hans Blumenberg, *The Legitimacy of the Modern Age* (Boston, MA: MIT Press, 1985).

6 On the theme of the Anthropocene let me suggest Bruno Latour, *Facing Gaia: Eight Lectures on the New Climatic Regime*; Bruno Latour, *After Lockdown: A Metamorphosis* (John Wiley & Sons, 2021); A. Vianello, "La sfida dell'Antropocene. L'impatto dell'uomo sulla storia della Terra," in *Studium*, 4 (2021): 540–62; and also some texts characterized by their more or less explicitly aesthetic features, such as Donna Haraway, *Staying with the Trouble: Making Kin in the Chthulucene* (Durham, NC: Duke University Press, 2016); D. Danowski and E. Viveiros de Castro, *Esiste un mondo a venire? Saggio sulle paure della fine*, Italian translation (Milan: Nottetempo, 2017); Timothy Morton, *Hyperobjects: Philosophy and Ecology after the End of the World* (Minneapolis, MN: University of Minnesota Press, 2013).

7 Reinhart Koselleck, *Futures Past: On the Semantics of Historical Time* (New York: Columbia University Press, 2004).

8 On this issue see above all Hans Joas, *The Power of the Sacred: An Alternative to the Narrative of Disenchantment* (Oxford, UK: Oxford University Press, 2021).

9 See Carl Schmitt, *Political Theology: Four Chapters on the Concept of Sovereignty*, trans. George Schwab (Chicago, IL: University of Chicago Press, 2005).

10 See Giorgio Agamben, *The Time That Remains: A Commentary on the Letter to the Romans* (Stanford, CA: Stanford University Press, 2005); Giorgio Agamben, *The Mystery of Evil: Benedict XVI and the End of Days* (Stanford, CA: Stanford University Press, 2017); Massimo Cacciari, *Dell'inizio* (Milan: Adelphi, 1990), 623–30;

Massimo Cacciari, *The Withholding Power: An Essay on Political Theology*, which contains a complete reconstruction of the event of the *katechon*; Roberto Esposito, "Cattolicesimo e modernità in Carl Schmitt", in Aa.Vv., *Tradizione e modernità nel pensiero politico di Carl Schmitt* (Napoli: Edizioni Scientifiche Italiane, 1987); Roberto Esposito, *Immunitas: The Protection and Negation of Life* (Cambridge, UK: Polity Press, 2011); Esposito, *Two: The Machine of Political Theology and the Place of Thought*. On the question of the *katechon* in relation to Croce with an eye toward the genesis of a "living thought" see Roberto Esposito, *Living Thought: The Origins and Actuality of Italian Philosophy* (Stanford, CA: Stanford University Press, 2012), 157.

11 These are terms employed by Giorgio Agamben in *The Kingdom and the Glory: For a Theological Genealogy of Economy and Government* (Stanford, CA: Stanford University Press, 2011).

12 See Agamben, *The Kingdom and the Glory*, 50–1.

13 Hans Belting, *Florence and Baghdad: Renaissance Art and Arab Science* (Cambridge, MA: Belknap Press of Harvard University Press, 2011).

14 Federico Vercellone, *L'archetipo cieco. Variazioni sull'individuo modern* (Torino: Rosenberg & Sellier, 2021).

15 See Massimo Cacciari, *The Withholding Power*.

16 Horst Bredekamp, *Leviathan: Body Politic as Visual Strategy in the Work of Thomas Hobbes* (Berlin: De Gruyter, 2020).

17 Johann Joachim Winckelmann, *Writings on Art* (New York: Phaidon, 1972), 72. For fundamental direction on the interpretation of this passage, see Peter Szondi, "Antico e moderno nell'estetica dell'età di Goethe" in *Poetica e filosofia della storia*, eds. R. Gilodi and F. Vercellone (Torino: Einaudi, 2001).

18 On this point see Federico Vercellone, *Nature del tempo. Novalis e la forma poetica del romanticismo Tedesco* (Milan: Guerini & Associati, 1998), chap. 1.

19 Obviously, it is fragment 116 of the *Athenaeum* which serves as a fundamental text. See Friedrich von Schlegel, *Philosophical Fragments* (Minneapolis, MN: University of Minnesota Press, 1991).

20 See Carl Schmitt, *Political Romanticism* (London: Routledge, 2017); and Carl Schmitt, *Roman Catholicism and Political Form* (Greenwood Publishing Group, 1996).

21 Schlegel, *Fragments*, 31–2.

22 See Koselleck, *Futures Past*.

23 See "Schopenhauer as Educator" in *Nietzsche: The Birth of Tragedy and Other Writings* (Cambridge, UK: Cambridge University Press, 1999), 146–55.

24 See *Carl Schmitt – Hans Blumenberg: Briefwechsel 1971–1978 und weitere Materialien*, eds. Alexander Schmitz and Marcel Lepper (Frankfurt: Suhrkamp, 2007).

Chapter Three

1 Keep in mind that the authenticity of this letter is contested: See, in the context of the most recent interpretations, Olivier Boulnois, *Saint Paul et la philosophie. Une introduction à l'essence du christianisme* (Paris: puf, 2022), 219–40.

2 On this point see Francesca Monateri, *Katechon. Filosofia, politica, estetica*.

3 See Barbara Carnevali, *Social Appearances. A Philosophy of Display and Prestige*, (New York: Columbia University Press, 2020).

4 On the proximity of kitsch and the sacred, see Marco Belpoliti and Gianfranco Marrone (eds.), "Kitsch," in *Riga*, 41 (2020).

5 On this issue, Erik Peterson engages polemically with Carl Schmitt. See Erik Peterson, "Der Monotheismus als politisches Problem" in *Theologische Traktate* (Würzburg, 1996).

6 This version of the letter of Paul comes from the Jerusalem Bible, Reader's Edition (Garden City, NY: Doubleday and Co., 1966), 266.

7 See Martin Hengel, *Zealots* (New York: Bloomsbury Academic, 1989).

8 See Jerome, "Ep. 121 to Algasia" in Andrew Cain, *The Letters of Jerome: Asceticism, Biblical Exegesis, and the Construction of Christian Authority in Late Antiquity* (Oxford, UK: Oxford University Press, 2009), 188–93; Irenaeus, "Against Heresies"

in Alexander Roberts, Sir James Donaldson, Arthur Cleveland Coxe, and Allan Menzies, *The Ante-Nicene Fathers: The Apostolic Fathers. Justin Martyr. Irenaeus* (C. Scribner's Sons, 1885), 309–566; F. Crawford Burkitt, *The Book of Rules of Tyconius* (Wipf and Stock Publishers, 2004).

9 Irenaeus, *Against Heresies*, 553.

10 Ibid., 554.

11 See Bruno Latour, *On the Modern Cult of the Factish Gods* (Chapel Hill, NC: Duke University Press, 2010).

12 Irenaeus, *Against Heresies*, 557.

13 Ibid., 558–9.

14 Burkitt, *The Book of Rules of Tyconius*, 67–8.

15 See Tertullian. *Tertullian: Apologetic and Practical Treatises* (Oxford, UK: J.H. Parker, 1842), 68–71.

16 Ibid., 82.

17 Ibid., 25–34.

18 Ibid., 70–1.

19 Ibid., 73–4.

20 Ibid., 72.

21 See above all Taubes, *Western Eschatology*, book 2; Saint Augustine (of Hippo), *The City of God Against the Pagans* (Cambridge, UK: Cambridge University Press, 1998), book 4.

22 St. Augustine, *The City of God Against the Pagans*, 143–85.

23 Ibid., 178.

24 Ibid., 223.

25 See Giovanni Filoramo, *Il sacro e il potere. Il caso cristiano* (Torino: Einaudi, 2009).

26 See Monateri, *Katechon*, paragraphs 2 and 3.

27 A fundamental resource is the book by Mondzain, *Image, Icon, Economy*.

28 On this topic see Pier Giuseppe Monateri, *L'augurio. Impero, legge e stato d'eccezione* (Milan-Udine: Mimesis, 2017).

29 See Federico Vercellone, "Archetipo cieco. Modelli della legittimazione estetico-politica," in *L'archetipo cieco*, 15–22.

30 Eusebius of Caesarea, *The Life of The Blessed Emperor Constantine [with the Oration of Constantine to the Assembly of Saints and the*

Oration of Eusebius in Praise of Constantine.], (London: Samuel Bagster and Sons, 1845), 297–8.

31 Ibid., 301–2.

32 See Giovanni Crisostomo, *In epistulam secundam ad Thessalonicenses Commentarius* iv, *homiliae 1–5*. See also Monateri, *Katechon*, chap. 1 par. 2.

33 On these themes see especially Filoramo, *Il sacro e il potere*, in particular, 31–78.

34 On this see in particular the fourth book of Augustine's *The City of God*.

35 Dante Alighieri, *Monarchy* (Cambridge, UK: Cambridge University Press, 1996), 28.

36 Martin Luther, *Ad librum eximii Magistri Nostri Magistri Ambrosii Catharini, defensoris Silvestri Prieriatis acerrimi, responsio.* 1521.

37 Luther, *Ad librum* … As Luther explains some pages before, *hidot* in Hebrew means: "problem, enigma, ambiguous discourse, which does not make sense if it is limited to appearances."

38 See Monateri, *Katechon*, chap. 2, par. 5.

Chapter Four

1 On this point I refer the reader again to my *L'archetipo cieco. Variazioni sull'individuo modern*.

2 Nicholas Berdyaev, *Dostoevsky*, trans. Donald Attwater (New York: Meridian Books, 1957), 201.

3 Vladimir Sergeyevich Solovyov, *War, Progress, and the End of History: Three Conversations, Including a Short Story of the Anti-Christ*, trans. Alexander Bakshy (London: University of London Press, 1915) 198–9.

4 Solovyov, *War, Progress, and the End of History*, 201.

5 See Francesca Monateri, *Katechon*, chap. 3, par. 1.

6 See Hoffmann, E.T.A. *The Devil's Elixir*, vol. 2 (Edinburgh: William Blackwood, 1824).

7 Vasiliĭ Vasilʹevich Rozanov and Василий Васильевич Розанов. *Dostoevsky and the Legend of the Grand Inquisitor* (Ithaca, NY: Cornell University Press, 1972), 128.

8 Ibid., 138.
9 Ibid., 150.
10 Ibid., 157–8.
11 Ibid., 166.
12 Ibid., 169.
13 Ibid., 183.
14 Ibid., 185–6.
15 See Monateri, *Katechon*, chap. 3, par. 3.
16 See Agamben, *The Kingdom and the Glory*, and Giorgio Agamben, *State of Exception: Homo Sacer II* (Chicago, IL: University of Chicago Press, 2008).
17 Hans Urs von Balthasar, *The Glory of the Lord: A Theological Aesthetics*, vol. 7 (San Francisco, CA: Ignatius Press, 1982–1990).
18 Agamben, *The Kingdom and the Glory*, 197.
19 See Roberto Esposito, *Two: The Machine of Political Theology*, 45–50, which refers not to the present situation but to the analysis Bataille gives to the charismatic leaders of fascism and Nazism.

Chapter Five

1 Massimo Cacciari, *The Withholding Power: An Essay on Political Theology*, trans. Ed Pucci (New York: Bloomsbury Publishing, 2018), 71–2.
2 Friedrich Wilhelm Nietzsche, *Thus Spoke Zarathustra*, trans. Adrian Del Caro (New York: Cambridge University Press, 2006), 9–10.
3 See Barbara Carnevali, *Social Appearances. A Philosophy of Display and Prestige* (New York: Columbia University Press, 2020).
4 Charles Taylor, *A Secular Age* (Cambridge, MA: Harvard University Press, 2007).
5 Marcel Gauchet, *The Disenchantment of the World: A Political History of Religion* (Princeton, NJ: Princeton University Press, 2021), 3.
6 Carl Gustav Jung, *The Archetypes and the Collective Unconscious* (Princeton, NJ: Princeton University Press, 1981).

7 Ernst Kantorowicz, *The King's Two Bodies: A Study in Medieval Political Theology* (Princeton University Press, 2016), 9.
8 Ibid., 15.
9 See Marie-Josè Mondzain, *Le Commerce des regards* (Paris: Seuil, 2003), 25. "Dès que le visible se substantialise, aussitôt l'image se meurt."
10 Ibid., chap. 1.
11 Ibid., 11.
12 Ibid., 73.
13 On this theme see Helga Nowotny and Giuseppe Testa. *Naked Genes: Reinventing the Human in the Molecular Age* (Boston, MA: MIT Press, 2011).
14 See Guy Debord, *The Society of the Spectacle*, trans. Donald Nicholson-Smith (Brooklyn, NY: Zone Books, 1994).
15 See Francesca Monateri, *Katechon*, chap. 1, par. 1.
16 Martin Heidegger, "The Age of the World Picture" in *Off the Beaten Track*, ed. and trans. Julian Young and Kenneth Haynes (Cambridge, UK: Cambridge University Press, 2002), 57–85.
17 See Jacob Taubes, "Carl Schmitt: Apocalyptic Prophet of the Counterrevolution" in *To Carl Schmitt: Letters and Reflections* (New York: Columbia University Press, 2013), 17–18.
18 See Walter Benjamin, *Toward the Critique of Violence: A Critical Edition* (Stanford, CA: Stanford University Press, 2021).
19 An absolutely fundamental text on this issue that has never been republished is Massimo Cacciari's *Krisis. Pensiero negativo e razionalizzazione da Nietzsche a Wittgenstein* (Milan: Feltrinelli, 1976).
20 Santiago Zabala, *Being at Large: Freedom in the Age of Alternative Facts* (Montreal: McGill-Queen's University Press, 2020).
21 See Carl Schmitt, *Roman Catholicism and Political Form* (Westport, CT: Greenwood Publishing Group, 1996).
22 See Schmitt, *Political Romanticism* (London: Routledge, 2017).
23 See Alexander Schmitz and Marcel Lepper (eds.), *Carl Schmitt – Hans Blumenberg: Briefwechsel 1971–1978*; and, of course, Blumenberg, *The Legitimacy of the Modern Age*.

24 Immanuel Kant, "What is Enlightenment?" in *On History*. Trans. L.W. Beck. (New York: MacMillan Publishing Company), 3.
25 Carl Schmitt, *Political Theology: Four Chapters on the Concept of Sovereignty*, trans. George Schwab (Chicago, IL: University of Chicago Press, 2005), 36.
26 Ibid., 59–60.
27 Ibid., 61 (translation slightly modified).
28 Ibid., 61.
29 Ibid., 66.
30 Ibid., 72.
31 Ibid., 70.
32 See Alexander Schmitz and Marcel Lepper (eds.), *Carl Schmitt – Hans Blumenberg: Briefwechsel 1971–1978*; Blumenberg, *The Legitimacy of the Modern Age*.
33 Carl Schmitt, *Glossarium: Aufzeichnungen Aus Den Jahren 1947 Bis 1958*, [fragment 11.1.48], 61. See also above, note 8 (Introduction).
34 Please allow me to refer the reader on this matter to my *Introduzione a Il nichilismo* (Rome-Bari: Laterza, 1992); see also, Costantino Esposito, *Il nichilismo del nostro tempo. Una cronaca* (Rome: Carocci, 2021).
35 See E.T.A Hoffmann, *Der Feind* (Würzburg: Königshausen & Neumann, 2002)
36 Jacob Taubes, *The Political Theology of Paul*, trans. Aleida Assmann (Stanford, CA: Stanford University Press, 2004), 103.
37 Water Benjamin, "Social Movement" in *The Arcades Project*, trans. Howard Eiland and Kevin McLaughlin (Cambridge, MA: Harvard University Press, 1999), 698–9.
38 See *Rouge. Art et utopie au pays des Soviets – Catalogue d'exposition* (Paris: Flammarion, 2019).
39 See Walter Benjamin, *On the Concept of History* (Createspace Independent Publishing Platform, 2016), 392. On the theme of an aesthetic of the ruins, allow me to refer the reader to my *Simboli della fine* (Bologna: il Mulino, 2018, chap. 7).

40 See Giovanni Gurisatti, "Nichilismo messianico e allegoria. Benjamin tra Schmitt e Taubes," in *Scenari*, 13, 2 (2020): 133–56, also for the framing of the theme in the debate which considers, beyond Schmitt and Taubes, Gershom Scholem. See also Elettra Stimilli, *Jacob Taubes. Sovranità e tempo messianico* (Brescia: Morcelliana, 2019).

41 Allow me to once again refer the reader on this matter to my *Introduzione a Il nichilismo*.

42 Walter Benjamin, *Reflections: Essays, Aphorisms, Autobiographical Writings*, trans. Edmund Jephcott (New York: Harcourt Brace Jovanovich, 1978), 313.

43 However, it should be remembered that Schmitt, almost anticipating the Cold War, refers to the *katechon* for the first time in reference to the United States, as Francesca Monateri recalls in *Katechon*, 25: "The first time the *katechon* appears is in *The Grossraum Order of International Law with a Ban on Intervention for Spatially Foreign Powers: A Contribution to the Concept of Reich in International Law* (1941)," in C. Schmitt, *Writings on War*, trans. T. Nunan (Cambridge: Polity Press, 2011) 75–124, "where Schmitt refers to the United States' choice to participate in the Second World War by presenting them as a *katechon*. Here Pauline power is conceived as an element that restrains universal historical development. In this sense, those who take on a catechonic role would limit themselves to clinging to a past in decline. The *katechon* therefore has no positive meaning; it is only a doting inability to grasp the times and serves only to delay the course of history." On the attribution and dating of Paul's letter cf. O. Metzger, "Il Katéchon. Una fondazione esegetica" in *Il Katéchon* (2 Thessalonians 2:6–7) *e l'anticristo. Teologia e politica di fronte al mistero dell'anomia* (Brescia, 1990), 33. But also J. Gabel, C. Wheeler, A.D. York, and D. Citino, *The Bible as literature: An Introduction*, 3rd edition (Oxford, UK: Oxford University Press, 2005), 210.

44 See Jacob Taubes, "Carl Schmitt: Apocalyptic Prophet of the Counterrevolution" in *To Carl Schmitt: Letters and Reflections* (New York: Columbia University Press, 2013), 1–18.

45 Ibid., 15.

46 In regard to the origins of the problem, allow me to refer the reader to my *Nature del tempo*.

47 Hans Belting, *An Anthropology of Images: Picture, Medium, Body* (Princeton, NJ: Princeton University Press, 2022).

48 See Paul Ricoeur, *Oneself as Another* (Chicago, IL: University of Chicago Press, 1992); Axel Honneth, *Recognition: A Chapter in the History of European Ideas* (Cambridge, UK: Cambridge University Press, 2020); Paolo Furia, *Rifiuto, altrove, utopia. Una fenomenologia estetica del riconoscimento nell'opera di Paul Ricoeur* (Milan-Udine: Mimesis, 2019).

49 See Cacciari, *The Withholding Power*, 114–5.

Chapter Six

1 This is what Giovanni Filoramo suggests in *Il sacro e il potere. Il caso Cristiano* (Torino: Einaudi, 2009), 63–4: "The Christ of the *Parousia* is, however, from a theological-political point of view, a figure of power, in fact of quintessential power, of power in its very foundation, of 'absolute' power. One might be tempted to say that, from the Christian point of view, if it is true that any power comes from God, this power is realized and grounded, by finding its representation and visibility only in the sovereignty of Christ."

2 See Horst Bredekamp, *Der schwimmende Souverän. Karl der Größe und die Bildpolitik des Körpers* (Berlin: Wagenbach, 2014).

3 On this topic see Mauro Menichetti, *Augusto e la teologia della Vittoria* (Rome: Quasar, 2021).

4 On this issue and in this context see Peter Sloterdijk, "The Anthropocene: A Stage in the Process on the Margins of the Earth's History?" in *What Happened in the Twentieth Century?: Toward a Critique of Extremist Reason* (Cambridge, UK: Wiley and Sons, 2018), 1–23.

5 See Sloterdijk, "The Anthropocene" and also Peter Sloterdijk, *Foams: Spheres Volume III: Plural Spherology* (Boston, MA: MIT Press, 2016).

6 See John 1, 15.

7 Ferdinand Tonnies, *Community and Society*, trans. Charles Price Loomis (Mineola, NY: Dover Publications, 2002).

8 Paul Ricoeur, *Time and Narrative*, vol. 2, trans. David Pellauer and Kathleen McLaughlin (Chicago: University of Chicago Press, 2012); Paul Ricoeur, *Oneself as Another*, trans. Kathleen Blamey (Chicago: University of Chicago Press, 1992); Paolo Furia, *Rifiuto, altrove, utopia. Una fenomenologia estetica del riconoscimento nell'opera di Paul Ricoeur* (Milan-Udine: Mimesis, 2019).

9 See Hans Joas, *The Power of the Sacred: An Alternative to the Narrative of Disenchantment* (Oxford, UK: Oxford University Press, 2021).

10 See Norbert Elias, "The Kitsch Style and the Age of Kitsch" in *Early Writings* (Dublin: University College of Dublin Press, 2005).

11 See Karl Kraus, "Brot und Lüge," in *Die Fackel*, xxi, 519/520 (1919): 25. On this see also Andrea Mecacci, *Il kitsch* (Bologna: il Mulino, 2014), 65.

12 Above all I am referring to Dwight Macdonald, *Masscult and Midcult: Essays Against the American Grain* (New York Review of Books, 2011).

13 See Mecacci, *il kitsch*, 108.

14 Rahel Jaeggi, *Critique of Forms of Life* (Cambridge, MA: Harvard University Press, 2018).

15 Edgar Morin, *Sur l'esthétique* (Paris: Éditions Robert Laffont, 2016).

16 See Salvatore Settis, *Serial/Portable Classic. Multiplaying Art in Greece and Rome*, in collaboration with A. Anguissola and D. Gasparotto (Milan: Fondazione Prada, 2015).

17 See Massimo Cacciari, *Hamletica* (Milan: Adelphi, 2009). Permit me to suggest again my *Archetipo cieco*.

18 See Theodor Adorno, "Kitsch" in *Essays on Music*, ed. Richard Leppert (Berkeley, CA: University of California Press, 2002), 501–5.

19 Hans-Georg Gadamer, *Gadamer on Celan: "Who Am I and Who Are You?" And Other Essays* (Albany, NY: SUNY Press, 1997).

20 Carl Schmitt, *Hamlet Or Hecuba: The Intrusion of the Time Into the Play* (Telos Press Pub., 2009).

21 Carl Gustav Jung, *The Archetypes and the Collective Unconscious* (Princeton, NJ: Princeton University Press, 1981), 15.

22 Friedrich von Schlegel, "Discourse on Mythology" in *Dialogue on Poetry and Literary Aphorisms* (Pennsylvania State University Press, 1968). On the theme see M. Cometa, *Iduna. Mitologie della ragione* (Palermo, Novecento, 1989).

23 This is the critique that Hegel directed at them, which is discussed in Pöggeler, *Hegels Kritik der Romantik*.

24 On this point see Chiara Simonigh and Federico Vercellone, "Pedro Al-modóvar e le rivoluzioni del simbolico," forthcoming from *Visual Culture Studies*.

25 See Marco Belpoliti, *Il corpo del capo* (Milano: Guanda, 2009).

26 On this see the essential work: Roberto Esposito, *Two: The Machine of Political Theology*.

27 Bernard Stiegler, *The Re-Enchantment of the World: The Value of Spirit Against Industrial Populism*, trans. Trevor Arthur (New York: Bloomsbury Academic, 2014). See also J.-J. Wunenburger, *Esthétique de la transfiguration* (Paris: Cerf, 2016), and J.-J. Wunenburger, "Bâtir, de l'ingénierie à la poiétique," in *Proposte per il reincantamento del mondo*, ed. F. Vercellone in *L'Ombra*, 12 (Bergamo: Moretti & Vitali, 2020), to be found within the first section.

28 See Carl Schmitt, *The Nomos of the Earth in the International Law of the Jus Publicum Europaeum*, trans. G.L. Ulmen (New York: Telos Press, 2006), 65–6.

29 See Giuliana Bruno, *Atlas of Emotion: Journeys in Art, Architecture, and Film* (New York: Verso, 2002).

30 For an entirely minority revaluation of ecstatic feeling within the aesthetic tradition see Morin, *Sur l'esthétique*.

31 See on this issue Emanuele Coccia, *The Life of Plants: A Metaphysics of Mixture* (Cambridge, UK: Polity Press, 2019); Emanuele Coccia, *Metamorphoses* (Cambridge, UK: Polity Press, 2021).

32 See Nicolas Bourriaud, *The Radicant*, trans. James Gussen and Lili Porten (Santa Monica, CA: Ram Publications, 2009).

33 See Walter Benjamin, "The Work of Art in the Age of Its Technological Reproducibility" in *Selected Writings: 1935–1938* (Cambridge, MA: Harvard University Press, 1996), 101–33.

34 Gernot Böhme, *The Aesthetics of Atmospheres*, ed. J.-P. Thibaud (London-New York: Routledge, 2017), chap. 12.

35 See Charles Taylor, *A Secular Age* (Cambridge, MA: Harvard University Press, 2007).

36 On the concept of niche see S. Tedesco, "Niche" in *Glossary of Morphology*, eds. Federico Vercellone, S. Tedesco (Cham: Springer, 2020), 355–8, e la bibliografia ivi riportata. See also K.N. Laland, T. Uller, M.W. Feldman, K. Sterelny, G.B. Müller, A. Moczek, E. Jablonka, J. Odling-Smee, "The extended evolutionary synthesis: Its structure, assumptions and predictions," in *Proceedings of the Royal Society B*, 282, 20151019 (2015): 1–14.

37 On the theme of the present state of community see Roberto Esposito, *Communitas: The Origin and Destiny of Community* (Stanford, CA: Stanford University Press, 2010).

38 See Marc Augé, *Non-Places: Introduction to an Anthropology of Supermodernity* (New York: Verso, 1995).

39 See Jaeggi, *Critique of Forms of Life*.

40 See Danilo Eccher, *Ettore Spalletti* (Milan: Skira, 2015).

41 Horst Bredekamp, *Image Acts. A Systematic Approach to Visual Agency* (Berlin-Boston: de Gryuter, 2017).

42 See S. Settis, *Incursioni. Arte contemporanea e tradizione* (Milano: Feltrinelli, 2020).

43 Regarding the theme of immersivity in history see O. Grau, *Virtual Art. From Illusion to Immersion* (Cambridge, MA: MIT Press, 2004).

44 On this theme see Ugo Perone, "The Public Space and Its Metaphors," *Symposium* 14 (2): 5–18; Ugo Perone (ed.), *Filosofia e spazio pubblico* (Bologna: il Mulino, 2012).

45 See, for an argument against the idea of anonymity, Alfred Gell, "The Technology of Enchantment and the Enchantment of Technology," in J. Coote (ed.), *Anthropology, Art and Aesthetics*

(Oxford, UK: Clarendon Press, 1984). See also Alfred Gell, *Art and Agency: An Anthropological Theory* (Oxford, UK: Clarendon Press, 1998).

46 On this point, allow me to refer the reader to the final chapter of *Oltre la bellezza* (Bologna: Il Mulino, 2008), 168–73.

47 See Giovanni Gentile, *The Philosophy of Art* (Ithaca, NY: Cornell University Press, 1972); and Paolo D'Angelo, *L'estetica italiana del Novecento. Dal neoidealismo a oggi* (Rome-Bari: Laterza 2007), chap. 2.

48 On this issue see Y. Michaud, *"L'art, c'est bien fini." Essai sur l'hyper-esthétique et les atmospheres* (Paris: Gallimard, 2021).

49 Paul Valéry, *Eupalinos: Or, The Architect*. Trans. William McCausland Stewart (Oxford, UK: Oxford University Press, 1932).

50 On the theme of a new humanism that takes advantage of the technological wave see Edgar Morin, *Pensare la complessità. Per un umanesimo planetario. Saggi critici e dialoghi di Edgar Morin con Gustavo Zagrebelsky e Gianni Vattimo*, ed. C. Simonigh (Milan-Udine: Mimesis, 2012); Mauro Ceruti and Francesco Bellusci, *Abitare la complessità. La sfida di un destino commune* (Milan-Udine: Mimesis, 2020).

Index